A MAN UNDER AUTHORITY

A Man
under
Authority

CHARLES SIBTHORPE

KINGSWAY PUBLICATIONS
EASTBOURNE

ISBN 0 86065 309 9

Unless otherwise indicated, biblical quotations are from
the New International Version, © New York International Bible
Society 1978.

AV = Authorized Version
crown copyright

Front cover design by Vic Mitchell

Printed in Great Britain for
KINGSWAY PUBLICATIONS LTD
Lottbridge Drove, Eastbourne, E. Sussex BN23 6NT by
Cox & Wyman Ltd, Reading
Typeset by Nuprint Services Ltd, Harpenden, Herts

Contents

*To my wife Joyce
and my children
Craig, Joanna, Daniel,
Coralie and Ben,
who are the first
to test the quality
of my life and leadership.*

Acknowledgements

I am grateful to God for the love and encouragement I have received in writing this book.

My special thanks to Marigold who has helped to make my thoughts intelligible, also to Sandy, David and Jane for their assistance. In particular I want to thank my family and household for their patience and encouragement—Joyce, Craig, Joanna, Daniel, Coralie, Ben, David, Lyn and Rosie.

I thank God for the Hyde Leaders' Week team where so much of the material for this book has been born and tested.

I praise God for Colin, Bob, David and Michael, my fellow elders in the Bethany Fellowship, where I seek to live out the reality of being 'a man under authority'.

I

Are You a Leader?

When Joyce and I were first married, our home was a large house which was a combination of a four-bedroomed dwelling and an old-fashioned grocery shop. One half became our home and the other was quickly turned into premises for our growing youth fellowship.

I was always interested in who would volunteer to clear up the coffee bar or give the place a coat of paint. It is interesting that those who were the most ready to serve took up positions of leadership later. One is now a missionary engaged in Bible translation in Africa, another is a church elder in the northeast, and one couple are house-group leaders in an Anglican church in Manchester.

Are you a servant?

One of the key principles of leadership is the willingness to be a servant. Jesus said: 'whoever wants to become great among you must be your servant, and whoever wants to be first must be your slave' (Mt 20:26–27).

Samuel had no aspirations to be a prophet when he served in the temple. It simply says of him: 'The boy Samuel ministered before the Lord under Eli' (1 Sam 3:1). God saw the trustworthy way in which he served and found his to be the only ears he could trust when he had a vital message that needed to be spoken to Eli. Greater responsibility was to follow.

When Elisha knew he was to succeed Elijah as God's prophet, his first responsibility was not to deliver a great message from God or to perform some miracle, but instead, as 1 Kings 19:21 says, 'He set out to follow Elijah and became his attendant.'

Every potential leader will be placed by God in situations of training through service and by performing simple, even menial, tasks. My friends in the youth fellowship began with a paintbrush in hand, Samuel by serving in the temple, and Elisha by attending Elijah.

Though serving is a vital preparation, it does not mean that all who serve are necessarily qualified to take up leadership among God's people. For this there must be a clear call from God.

Are you called by God?

I will always remember the day God called me into full-time ministry. It happened in a small chapel in Cornwall, at St Agnes Beacon. Dr Denis Ball had been invited to speak at a series of meetings in this isolated country chapel. When I arrived with Joyce and a car-load of friends I was appalled at the poor attendance, and spent the first half of the service feeling angry that there were not more people present. However, when Denis began to speak I realized that God had only drawn together a few because he had a particular message for us.

God was calling me to commit my life in obedience and service in a way I had never done before, and as Denis invited people to come forward for prayer, I leapt from my chair and was first at the front. I knew that it was important for me to act quickly, even though I would have found it more natural to have waited for others and followed them. But God had called and I had to be obedient to that call.

The initiative always belongs to God. Jeremiah was called by God, despite his youth and his fears. 'See, today I appoint you over nations and kingdoms to uproot and tear down, to destroy and overthrow, to build and to plant' (Jer 1:10).

God calls those whom *he* chooses. Therefore it is never a light responsibility to be chosen for leadership. God will always confirm his call, made initially to the individual, by speaking again through the Scriptures and through the affirmation of other Christians within the body of Christ.

Do you feel reticent?

When a leader knows he is not capable of fulfilling his work in his own strength, there will always be a personal reluctance to go on. This is not a false humility, but a genuine reticence born from the honest knowledge of his own human limitations.

Human reticence is found in many of Paul's writings because he knew he could only exercise his leadership under God's authority and with his power. Natural words and actions will not produce supernatural results in people's lives, as the gospel is a supernatural work of God and can only be activated through daily living faith. Paul's description of his mission to Corinth makes this very clear: 'When I came to you, brothers, I did not come with eloquence or superior wisdom as I proclaimed to you the testimony about God. For I resolved to know nothing while I was with you except Jesus Christ and him crucified. I came to you in weakness and fear, and with much trembling' (1 Cor 2:1–3).

Moses, when he received God's call to leadership, said: 'O Lord, please send someone else to do it.' I do like the honesty and frankness of the Bible narrative. It shows one of the secrets of Moses' greatness. In short, he never got too big for his boots!

Gideon's response to his call was similar: 'But Lord, how can I save Israel? My clan is the weakest in Manasseh, and I am the least in my family.'

Right at the end of Paul's second letter to Corinth we find a pithy statement that recognizes the key to spiritual power: 'When I am weak, then I am strong' (2 Cor 12:10).

Do you speak the word?

'Remember your leaders, who spoke the word of God to you' (Heb 13:7). There is no shortage of words in today's church. How many of them are effective? Jesus said to his disciples: 'The words I say to you are not just my own' (Jn 14:10). Jesus only spoke the words that God gave him. He also said:

'The words I have spoken to you are spirit and they are life' (Jn 6:63).

Human reason has a very limited effect and only lasts until someone produces a better and more convincing argument, but to speak the word God gives has life-transforming power. God's word brings salvation to lost humanity, it brings power into the vacuum of human weakness and healing to broken and sick bodies.

Paul said: 'My message and my preaching were not with wise and persuasive words, but with a demonstration of the Spirit's power, so that your faith might not rest on men's wisdom, but on God's power' (1 Cor 2:4–5).

It is therefore important that a leader is a man of God's word. Such a man will have a thorough knowledge of the Bible, his life will be in harmony with its teaching and his words will bear the stamp of God's authority.

Paul told Timothy: 'Do your best to present yourself to God as one approved, a workman who does not need to be ashamed and who correctly handles the word of truth' (2 Tim 2:15).

Do you live your message?

'Remember your leaders…. Consider the outcome of their way of life' (Heb 13:7). There are people in our society today who are leaders in business, commerce and politics, serving well in spite of the fact that their personal lives are in disarray. They are able to live their lives in compartments, so that one part does not seriously affect the other. A man may have a successful business with all his employees well paid and sensitively cared for, while at home his marriage is breaking up as a result of his own lack of concern at a personal level.

A spiritual leader cannot operate in this way and be effective. 'Consider the outcome of their way of life'. Life speaks more powerfully than words. This does not mean that all that is spoken or preached is valueless unless perfection has been reached in the speaker's life, but it does mean that a man will apply the word of God to himself first and only then will he be at liberty to share it with others.

So the exciting truth is this: the more I allow God to do *in* me, the more he will be able to do *through* me.

Jesus said: 'If anyone would come after me, he must deny himself and take up his cross daily and follow me' (Lk 9:23). To be living the life of Jesus is to say 'goodbye' to the life of self.

Paul was bold enough to say: 'Therefore I urge you to imitate me' (1 Cor 4:16). In fact whether he said it or not, that is exactly what those who respected him would do, for at all levels of morality and lifestyle a man reproduces himself in those whom he is called to lead. This is most easily seen in the way children are affected by their parents.

Paul goes on to say: 'For this reason I am sending to you Timothy, my son whom I love, who is faithful in the Lord. He will remind you of my way of life in Christ Jesus, which agrees with what I teach everywhere in every church' (1 Cor 4:17).

The standards are high but not impossible. Peter writes about the resources that God gives to enable us to live as he intended: 'His divine power has given us everything we need for life and godliness through our knowledge of him who called us by his own glory and goodness' (2 Pet 1:3).

Do you operate by faith?

'Remember your leaders…and imitate their faith' (Heb 13:7). Another distinct contrast between leaders in society and business and spiritual leaders is that whereas the former can operate purely out of experience and training, a leader of God's people must be a man of faith.

The activity of faith brings the mighty power of God into every situation of life and worship. In Hebrews 11:6 it says: 'And without faith it is impossible to please God, because anyone who comes to him must believe that he exists and that he rewards those who earnestly seek him.'

So as we look at a Christian leader we will expect to see a quality of faith that is infectious, a faith that we want to imitate. Faith points to God who has control of every detail of our lives and who, although understanding the difficulties we may be experiencing, desires to bring his resources to change those circumstances.

Paul said in Romans 1:17—'For in the gospel a righteousness from God is revealed, a righteousness that is by faith from first to last, just as it is written: "The righteous will live by faith".'

Faith is needed to lead people from the darkness of sin to the new birth that is in Jesus.

Faith is needed to minister the power of the Holy Spirit into lives that are defeated and powerless.

It is by faith that the sick are prayed for and healed in the name of Jesus.

It is by faith that the powers of darkness are smashed and people are released into the glorious freedom that is in Christ Jesus.

It is by faith that everyday situations are brought from defeat and discouragement into victory and joy.

Are you followed?

Jesus said: 'Come, follow me…and I will make you fishers of men.' Then we are told: 'At once they left their nets and followed him' (Mk 1:17–18).

When I was in business in Cornwall we had three stores and employed about seventy people. As a manager I was obeyed and felt that I had a loyal and hardworking staff. That was encouraging and flattering to my leadership and business skills. But the fact is that I was paying these people for the work being done. If I had stopped the money, the responsiveness would have disappeared rapidly.

Leadership within the body of Christ is different. The people are not being paid and are not under any compulsion to submit. Leadership on the one hand and submission on the other are vital, but the whole dynamic is based on the relationship between God and man, not on reward.

A leader needs to give a strong lead and his life needs to be in line with God's word. His leadership will be tested by the way in which people respond to it. This does not mean that he should try to please the people. Not at all! If he is a man-pleaser he will have moved out from under God's authority and will not be worth following.

Judges 5:2 (RSV) says: 'That the leaders took the lead in Israel, that the people offered themselves willingly, bless the Lord!'

If no one is following, then the man is not a leader. But if his life clearly bears the stamp of God then there will be people who will offer themselves willingly.

Are you fruitful?

When an orchard of apple trees is planted, a harvest of delicious and tasty apples will be the expectation. God 'plants' or appoints leaders with the anticipation of reaping a rich harvest of fruit in the lives of his people. Paul referred to certain of his followers as his 'dear children, for whom I am again in the pains of childbirth until Christ is formed in you' (Gal 4:19).

Fruitfulness in God's people is the reflection of Christ in their lives. Others may pick and be nourished by this fruit. Jesus said: 'You did not choose me, but I chose you to go and bear fruit—fruit that will last' (Jn 15:16).

But fruitfulness is primarily for God. 'Live as children of light (for the fruit of the light consists in all goodness, righteousness and truth) and find out what pleases the Lord' (Eph 5:9–10).

God is eager to give us the gift of his Holy Spirit which bears fruit that glorifies him and is a blessing to others. 'But the fruit of the Spirit is love, joy, peace, patience, kindness, goodness, faithfulness, gentleness and self-control' (Gal 5:22–23).

Of course it is essential that a leader is himself a person who is bearing fruit and this will be seen in the way that God is at work in the lives of the people under him. The fruit will be distinct and visible. The unconverted will find Christ as Saviour and Lord; the weak and defeated will be strengthened in the word and by the power of God's Spirit. People will say 'God is here' because they can see him at work among his people.

Are you ahead of the people?

This may seem to be a strange question. But you need to be ahead of your people if you are to be followed. Paul was bold enough to say: 'Follow my example, as I follow the example of Christ' (1 Cor 11:1).

Leaders live under the responsibility of continually pressing on with God. This is not to say that every leader will be a spiritual giant, you need only be half a pace in front of the people. God will lead you step by step and you will bring the people on in the same way, step by step. To be a leader means that you have been called by God and are ready to forge ahead with him. It is often a lonely path, because you are breaking new ground for others to walk through later, but you yourself will only be following in the way that Jesus has already trodden.

Through discouragement and fatigue, leaders often find they have not remained out in front and so their people have come to a standstill. Sometimes a man will say: 'My people have stopped moving on with God, they are stuck.' The truth of the matter is that their leader is stuck.

It is this situation more than any other that brought about the concept behind the Leaders' Weeks at The Hyde, which is the main thrust of my own ministry.

Hyde Leaders' Weeks

As I travelled around the country as part of a team leading missions in various towns, I became aware of ministers and leaders who were working tirelessly and faithfully and yet needed a fresh touch from God. I knew that God had spoken to us in the Bethany Fellowship about encouraging leaders and ministers as part of his calling to us.

In 1982 it became clear that the way was open for this work to begin. God laid the burden for this ministry upon my heart and, despite a sense of great personal inadequacy, my fellow elders Colin Urquhart and Bob Gordon encouraged me to pursue the vision, and agreed to share in the teaching.

The Leaders' Week brochure states the purpose of a

Leaders' Week:

- a new meeting with God;
- a renewed sense of the power of the Spirit;
- a new release into ministry;
- a new vision for the future.

Fourteen of these Weeks are held each year when around twenty-five ministers, elders, leaders and their wives gather at The Hyde for a week of seeking God. The Bethany Fellowship is centred on The Hyde, a country house at Handcross, Sussex. People arrive on Monday afternoon and the Week ends mid-morning on Friday. This allows adequate time for travelling without interfering with home responsibilities at weekends. Accommodation is provided at The Hyde itself and in the homes of Fellowship members living close by.

The emphasis is on personal revival and the inner working of God in each person's life, so that as his life is transformed by God, so his ministry will be released into new power.

It is out of the context of these Weeks that this book is written.

A man under authority

The title of this book is not intended to confine its readership to men only! It is taken straight from the story of the healing of the centurion's servant in Matthew 8 which states the essence of Christian leadership—that we exercise authority on behalf of Another. The more of God's authority there is in your life, the more of his authority will be released through you into the lives of others.

This book is for all who are called to leadership within the body of Christ—men and women, clergy and ministers, elders and deacons, house-group leaders, youth workers, leaders of praise and worship—in fact, any person who by quiet diligence as well as divine call is being used by God to minister his life and power.

The basic principle that applies throughout is that leaders lead by example. As God works *in* you, he will then be able to work *through* you.

PART 1

The Quality of a Leader's Life

2

A Man with a Heart after God

I was in my car driving up the M6 and listening to Andrae Crouch's *Live in London* concert album. The volume was turned up and I was reliving the experience of having been at that concert myself.

The sound was washing over me and I was enjoying the vibrancy and energy of the music. A loud and rhythmic track had just finished and there was a bit of chat before a softer, quieter song began. It was all about love for God. The lyrics were powerful.

The song was speaking to me in a way that it had never done before, in spite of the fact that I had listened to it many times. The line that really got through to me was this: 'You can take the one I love, I love the best…but I'm going to keep on loving you Lord.' Before I could take a grip on myself I found that I was crying, and although there was no one else in the car I felt embarrassed. Questions were racing through my mind. Can I really identify with that statement? Do I mean, Lord, that if you were to take my wife Joyce in death, or one of the children, that I would continue to love you just as much?

I tussled with the questions as I drove on through the afternoon sunshine. Do I really mean it? I rewound the cassette, played it again, and pondered the questions once more. Deep within me I knew that the answer was: 'Yes, Lord,' even though that response had not been put to the test.

A heart after God

The people of Israel had asked for a king: Saul had been made king. He had started well, but as the pressures of office increased, the flaws in his character became apparent. God did not have first place in his heart and he became prey to all kinds of influences. Eventually he disobeyed God and took it upon himself to sacrifice the burnt offering, which was an act only to be performed by the priest. He had failed to follow in the ways of God so he was set aside and lost his kingdom.

As Samuel pronounced judgement on Saul, he emphasized the quality that God required in the new king: 'But now your kingdom will not endure; the Lord has sought out a man after his own heart and appointed him leader of his people' (1 Sam 13:14).

The contrast between Saul and David is interesting—both of them sinned and failed, but whereas Saul was rejected and set aside by God, David came through to restoration and forgiveness. What made the difference?

Saul was full of self-justification when Samuel confronted him with his sin (1 Sam 15:13–35), and even his attempted repentance was tainted with self-protection as he said, 'I have sinned. But please honour me before the elders of my people' (v.30).

Saul's love was centred upon himself and self-pleasing; 1 Chronicles 10:13 writes his epitaph thus: 'Saul died because he was unfaithful to the Lord; he did not keep the word of the Lord.' His self-love meant that he would always be unreliable in the face of difficulties and it was this that led to his final rejection and loss of kingship.

In contrast, David, when faced with his adultery and murder, said, 'I have sinned against the Lord' (2 Sam 12:13). His love was centred upon God and the pain of how his sin displeased God is evident in Psalm 51: 'Do not cast me from your presence' (v.11); 'Save me from bloodguilt, O God' (v.14); 'The sacrifices of God are a broken spirit; a broken and contrite heart, O God, you will not despise' (v.17).

Leaders do experience sin and failure that can jeopardize their future. God is always willing to redeem situations when there is true repentance. The focus of love is revealed in the face of sin and stress.

So David was chosen and anointed by God as the next monarch. God knew that when David was under pressure the quality of his relationship with him would show through. The psalms of David speak eloquently of his love and devotion for God: 'I love you, O Lord, my strength. The Lord is my rock, my fortress and my deliverer; my God is my rock, in whom I take refuge' (Ps 18:1–2).

When the going gets tough, your actions will reveal where you have really placed your love and trust. Your love for God is vital. This is illustrated in the story of the twelve men who were sent by Moses to spy out the land of Canaan. They all saw the same things, yet the reaction of Joshua and Caleb was so different from the rest. Why? Because they had entered into a relationship with God which released faith and confidence within them. The despondent reaction of the other spies showed that the circumstances had a more powerful influence upon them than the faithfulness of God. God makes his own comment on Caleb when he says: 'my servant Caleb has a different spirit and follows me wholeheartedly' (Num 14:24).

C. T. Studd, the famous pioneer missionary, expressed his commitment to God in these words: 'If Jesus Christ be God and died for me, then no sacrifice can be too great for me to make for him.' This is plainly the declaration of a man whose heart is after God.

Love for God releases God's presence into life and work

Love for God is at the centre of the Bible's teaching. The one who has captured your heart motivates your whole life. Jesus said: 'For out of the overflow of his heart his mouth speaks' (Lk 6:45).

God knew the things that would compete for the hearts of mankind. That is why he gave such a direct command to his covenant people when he said to them: 'Love the Lord your God with all your heart and with all your soul and with all your strength' (Deut 6:5).

The things that dominate your heart will dominate your thoughts, and your thoughts will dominate your life. What you are deep inside before a holy God who knows all about you will be what you produce in your life and work. The fruit you see in the lives of others around you will be a reflection of what is coming out of your own life, and as you lead, you reproduce yourself in the lives of those who are influenced by you. It is not so much what you say that affects others, but what you are.

Perhaps you know someone who is completely crazy about football. He eats, lives and sleeps football. Anyone who comes within earshot of him will be told all the latest news about his favourite football team. His clothes, the decor of his bedroom, the stickers on his car all tell the same story. No one is in any doubt: that which has captured his heart motivates his life. His lifestyle will either attract or repel, but those who remain in the sphere of his influence will become infected by his love for football.

If love for the church supplants love for God you may well produce churchianity (love for church) instead of Christianity (love for Christ).

Does the choir bring worshippers into the living presence of God, or does it bring the glory that is God's alone upon itself? Are the musicians more taken up with their instruments, be they guitars or organ pipes, than they are with the living God? Is the youth group an end in itself or is it the means of introducing other young people to a vibrant faith in Jesus?

As you look at your work for God, you will be able to see clearly the strengths and weaknesses of your whole life. Just as the love and presence of God should be experienced as people come into your home, so also should the love of God be felt by those coming into contact with your leadership.

Love for God brings obedience to his word

Jesus said: 'If anyone loves me, he will obey my teaching' (Jn 14:23). It is important to check out the depth of your love for God by looking carefully at the extent of your obedience.

Love that goes deep will touch the emotions, but it will go beyond that to determine behaviour. It is not a sign of weakness to be so overwhelmed by love for God that tears are shed. Nor is it unseemly to be so in love with Jesus that you are 'lost in wonder, love and praise'. True love for God will be warm, and will be expressed in joy and abandonment during times of worship and praise, and in a life that is marked by its obedience to the teachings of Jesus.

That does not mean following a legalistic code of religious rules, a practice of the Pharisees that was firmly condemned by Jesus. It does mean joyful obedience to all that Jesus taught.

In John's first letter he describes obedience in two different ways: he says that when praying with faith we can receive from God anything we ask, because (a) we obey his commands, and (b) we do what pleases him (1 Jn 3:21–22). What is the difference between the two?

To answer that question let me give an illustration from my own life. At about nine o'clock in the evening when I am at home, sitting with my household around the fire, I will ask: 'Who is going to make us all a drink?' This will precipitate a discussion among both children and adults as to whose turn it is and who is willing to undertake this mighty act of service. Eventually someone volunteers, and my question has been answered with obedience as the result. Sometimes one of the children, usually the same one, will offer, without being asked, to make everyone a cup of coffee. We all respond and it is not long before we have been served.

The first example is merely an act of obedience, the second is the service of love.

How much of your behaviour is the expression of your love for God?

Love for God brings security in life and confidence in ministry

How do you arrive at the place where you know your love for God is the most powerful force in the whole of your life?

One of the reasons why your love for God is not as strong

as you would want is because you have not fully received the love God has for you. You need love from God in order to love him. You need love from God in order to love others. Natural human love will be inadequate on both counts.

Receive the love of God into your heart and know without a doubt that he has chosen you and has made you his son or daughter. Many people have complete assurance that they have received new life and salvation in Christ and yet have no deep understanding or confidence that they are really loved by God.

Insecurity is one of the most powerful of emotions, and it can weaken and undermine your relationships, both with God and man. The healing of insecurities comes not so much from understanding the hurts and pains of childhood, but by a revelation that you are loved and accepted by God today.

John says: 'We love because he first loved us' (1 Jn 4:19), and 'How great is the love the Father has lavished on us, that we should be called children of God! And that is what we are!' (1 Jn 3:1).

God has chosen you because he loves you; because he loves you he has made you one of the family; and that means that you belong to him and he belongs to you!

How then can you possibly feel insecure? Well, the enemy of your soul wants to put lies into your mind that go something like this: 'I know God loves all mankind, but he cannot possibly love me. I can understand why he chose others, but I know he does not really want me.'

You may wonder how it is that that sentence could possibly occur in a book on Christian leadership. Let me tell you that leaders are among the most insecure people I have met. Many are working day and night because they feel so unloved and uncertain of God's care for them. They feel that if they work hard enough and serve others selflessly enough, then they will earn his love and approval.

That is a tragedy, because there is no way you can earn anything from God. What you are and what you shall become is entirely dependent upon his grace and love. You can merit none of his favour. Endeavouring to do so proves counterproductive to God's real purposes: your own restlessness and doubt is spread rather than the peace and love of God.

During a recent Hyde Leaders' Week I was speaking to a minister whose life had been a catalogue of failure and rejection. Despite that, God had definitely called him to ministry and leadership. He had a very real love for God and for his people. But because of deep insecurities he found it impossible to pastor his people personally. His expectation was that they would reject both his ministry and himself: this thought left him paralysed with fear. I explained that God wanted to heal all past hurts and rejection, and release into his life such a powerful revelation of God's love and acceptance that a new ministry based on the firm foundation of God's love would begin to flow out through him.

We prayed together and he forgave all those who had contributed to the damage of the past and asked forgiveness for his own lack of faith and trust in a loving God. Then in the name of Jesus he was released from all that had been destructive in his past life. He received the promise that he had been redeemed from the empty way of life handed down to him from his forefathers (1 Pet 1:18–19). I asked God to give a revelation by his Spirit of the love, acceptance and healing he had given to this child of his. The effect was dramatic and powerful and I praise God that this man is now able to minister the salvation, power and love of Jesus to others.

One of the reasons why you need to know the present reality of being filled with the Holy Spirit is 'because those who are led by the Spirit of God are sons of God. For you did not receive a spirit that makes you a slave again to fear, but you received the Spirit of sonship. And by him we cry "Abba, Father". The Spirit himself testifies with our spirit that we are God's children' (Rom 8:14–16).

If you neglect the work of the Holy Spirit, your ministry will become cold and lifeless. You may be bringing people into a Christian system, but are you introducing them to the living, loving Father? The reality of our faith is that it is spiritual and supernatural. Therefore, the knowledge of salvation comes by the work of the Holy Spirit. The power to live your life as God's child comes through the infilling of the Holy Spirit. The revelation of God's love and fatherhood is also by the Holy Spirit.

Luther once said: 'The longest journey in the world is from a man's head to his heart.' I know that my belief in Christ took that 15-inch journey when God filled me with his Holy Spirit.

Love for God dispels fear and deals with human pressure

'There is no fear in love. But perfect love drives out fear' (1 Jn 4:18). Love for God is so important: it can control other forces that seek to manipulate our lives. Your love, the all-consuming passion in your life, will regulate the way in which other people and events can impinge upon you.

'Fear of man will prove to be a snare' (Prov 29:25); 'The fear of the Lord is the beginning of wisdom' (Prov 9:10). Your love for God and the revelation of his love for you need to be the most powerful forces in your life. Then you will not be prey to every pressure put upon you by the people whom you are leading, because the power of the love of God will control your thoughts and actions. You will be set free to hear God, to obey him and to lead those people to know and love God.

What is the depth of your love for God? Do you really know how great God's love is for you? Will the strength of your love for him and the power of his love for you keep your life strong in the face of all opposition?

You need to know the answers to those questions. Jesus needed to know the depth of Peter's response. That is why he was so persistent in the encounter recorded in John 21:15–18.

'Simon son of John, do you truly love me more than these?' 'Yes Lord,' he said, 'you know that I love you.' Jesus said, 'Feed my lambs.' Again Jesus said, 'Simon son of John, do you truly love me?' He answered, 'Yes, Lord, you know that I love you.' Jesus said, 'Take care of my sheep.' The third time he said to him 'Simon son of John, do you love me?' Peter was hurt because Jesus asked him the third time, 'Do you love me?' He said, 'Lord, you know all things; you know that I love you.' Jesus said, 'Feed my sheep. I tell you the truth, when you were younger you dressed yourself and went where you wanted; but when you are old you will stretch out your hands, and someone else will dress you and lead you where you do not want to go.'

It was of the utmost importance that both Jesus and Peter knew the extent of their love for each other. As far as Jesus was concerned that was not in doubt, but Peter's love had been tested already and been found wanting. The questions were clear and penetrating, and the answers were honest. This was not only the prelude to mighty blessing for thousands on the day of Pentecost, but it also led to great personal cost for Peter and eventual martyrdom in the cause of Christ.

I believe God is looking for men and women today who will give themselves wholeheartedly to love and serve him and to be his anointed leaders. It is a costly and demanding commitment, as was Peter's, and requires a love and perseverance so strong that they will stop at nothing for the sake of the Lord.

3

A Man Who Stands before God

I have often been amused by a story Colin Urquhart tells
from his parish experience at Luton. Colin became so involved with the personal problems and needs of his congregation that by the time Saturday night came he could think of
nothing else. Everything within him wanted to stand up in
the pulpit on Sunday and sort the people out! But was this
what God wanted?

Colin found a way of dealing with the situation. He would
go into the church, lock the door and climb into the pulpit.
He would view the empty pews and, with a mental picture of
all the people who would fill them the next day, he would
speak out just what they needed to hear! Having got it all out
of his system, Colin would then step down from the pulpit,
sink to his knees at the altar rail and cry out: 'All right, Lord,
now what do *you* want to say?'

When recounting this story at a leaders' meeting, Colin
usually adds this important statement: 'If you minister to the
Lord, he will minister to the people.'

What is 'ministry' and what does it mean to 'minister'? It
means service and to be a servant. There is nothing exalted
about being a minister—it simply means being willing to
take the lowest place. Jesus said: 'The Son of Man did not
come to be served, but to serve, and to give his life as a
ransom for many' (Mt 20:28). It is a privilege to be chosen by
God and to be entrusted with his life-changing word. A
servant of God is obedient to him and serves others on his
behalf. Paul preferred to call himself a slave: 'Though I am
free and belong to no man, I make myself a slave to everyone,
to win as many as possible' (1 Cor 9:19).

Ministering to the Lord

A vital principle of Christian leadership is that we are called primarily to stand before the Lord and to minister to him. In the early books of the Bible, this principle is seen in the work of the levitical priests. 'At that time the Lord set apart the tribe of Levi to carry the ark of the covenant of the Lord, to stand before the Lord to minister and to pronounce blessings in his name, as they still do today' (Deut 10:8).

The sobering fact is this: unless ministry is pleasing to God it will be powerless. Are you in leadership to please God, to please the people or to please yourself? That question needs careful consideration.

Unless you acknowledge the fact that you are called by God to stand in his holy presence every day and to worship and serve him, you will fall victim to all the pressures of life. How foolish to become wrapped up in a world of problems and lose sight of the majestic awesomeness of God.

Repentance leads to a new responsiveness

When Isaiah went into the temple 'in the year that King Uzziah died' (Is 6), he must have been puzzled by the sad end of a king who had been greatly used by God. Why had Uzziah disobeyed God by burning incense in the temple, which was a privilege reserved solely for the priests? Why had God struck him down with leprosy? That seemed a very severe punishment. Had Isaiah felt aggrieved with God, it would be easy to sympathize with him; but Isaiah did not argue or reason with God. He went into the temple to worship him and to stand in his presence.

Isaiah recalled, 'I saw the Lord seated on a throne, high and exalted' (v.1) and then went on to describe the majestic scene before him. When you are facing situations that you cannot understand and are looking for answers where there seem to be none, God holds the key. His holy presence did not give human answers but it transformed Isaiah's whole perspective on life. As one involved in ministry you need constantly to withdraw from the hurly-burly and demands of your work to spend time alone with God.

Isaiah was so overwhelmed by the greatness and glory of God that a dramatic transformation took place. The vision of a holy God caused him to acknowledge his unholiness and utter weakness. 'Woe to me,' he cried. 'I am ruined! for I am a man of unclean lips' (6:5).

Isaiah's repentance released God's forgiveness and cleansing. The seraph flew to the altar, removed the live coal and touched Isaiah's mouth saying, 'See, this has touched your lips; your guilt is taken away and your sin atoned for' (v.7).

Following all this, God spoke directly to him. 'Whom shall I send? And who will go for us?' (v.8). God's love is always towards the lost, and he is constantly searching for those who have counted the cost and are ready to be called out. When a man has met with God in such a profound way, he will have shared something of God's heart of compassion for those who are 'without hope and without God in the world' (Eph 2:12). Isaiah's response was immediate: 'Here am I. Send me!' (v.8).

Consistency results in maturity

At The Hyde Leaders' Weeks, ministers and leaders often arrive discouraged and battered by the circumstances they have left behind. We do not attempt initially to look for the answers to these problems, but to point to the living God. Often, when a man has stood before God and had a fresh encounter with him, he will know the answer to his dilemma. To stand before God and hear his voice more clearly than the voice of man is to be reassured by his love and peace, whatever the situation. It will provide protection from the erosive effects of the surrounding sin and darkness.

The story of Samuel from the Old Testament is a powerful illustration. It begins with the charming account of Hannah praying for the gift of a baby boy, and then reveals how she gave the child back to God when her prayer had been answered.

The environment of Samuel's training for ministry (1 Sam 2) was far from ideal. Eli was very old and had lost his grip on the job. His two sons Hophni and Phinehas were living lives of sin and disobedience to God.

'They had no regard for the Lord' (v.12); 'This sin of the young men was very great in the Lord's sight, for they were treating the Lord's offering with contempt' (v.17); 'they slept with the women who served at the entrance to the Tent of Meeting' (v.22).

How did all this affect Samuel? Surely no one could stand firm and develop spiritual stature under such conditions. But Samuel did, and his secret lay in three phrases from that same chapter: 'but the boy ministered before the Lord under Eli the priest' (v.11); 'But Samuel was ministering before the Lord' (v.18); 'Meanwhile, the boy Samuel grew up in the presence of the Lord' (v.21).

To stand before God with consistency leads to maturity: 'And the boy Samuel continued to grow in stature and in favour with the Lord and with men' (v.26).

Humility develops sensitivity

'The boy Samuel ministered before the Lord under Eli' (1 Sam 3:1a). Although Samuel was young, he could have reacted against the sin that he saw around him by disobeying Eli's authority or by complaining to his parents during their annual visit. But instead, he submitted his life in humility to the authority God had placed over him, and as a result his life bore fruit for the Lord.

'In those days the word of the Lord was rare; there were not many visions' (1 Sam 3:1b). Disobedience, impurity and spiritual darkness will prevent the voice of God being heard and will leave men making merely human decisions. If a leader fails to stand before God in humility he will not hear the still small voice (1 Kings 19:12 RSV); instead he will be dominated by other voices. The voice of reason, of compromise, of self-protection, or even the voice of the people, will vie for his attention.

The result of Samuel's humility under human authority and the development of his own relationship with God, was that he was ready to receive the message that was to come from God (1 Sam 3:9).

'The Lord was with Samuel as he grew up, and he let none of his words fall to the ground' (1 Sam 3:19). When a man has learned to listen to God and has developed spiritual sensitivity, God will continue to speak to him and he will grow in authority. 'The Lord continued to appear at Shiloh, and there he revealed himself to Samuel through his word. And Samuel's word came to all Israel' (1 Sam 3:21).

Dependence encourages intercession and faith

What do you do when you are faced with an impossible situation? That is what confronted Abraham. He had already taken a great step of faith when he was told that Sarah was to have a child. Then the Lord told him that he was going to examine the state of Sodom and Gomorrah because of its great sinfulness. Abraham knew the situation already and it was grim. The men who had brought the good news that Sarah was going to conceive a child were already on their way to Sodom. What should Abraham do? Should he hurry to Sodom and try to preach a message of righteousness to the people? Should he discuss the situation with Lot? He did neither of these: 'but Abraham remained standing before the Lord' (Gen 18:22).

A leader who stands before God in dependence upon him is a man of prayer and a man of faith. If a prayer meeting has been replaced by a committee meeting, the wrong gathering has been cancelled. It is amazing to witness reactions to the suggestion that a church council or meeting of deacons should spend its entire meeting in prayer. Have you ever given a leadership meeting entirely over to prayer?

I will always remember a particular meeting of one of the leadership groups of the Bethany Fellowship. David Brown, one of the elders, was responsible for the pastoral oversight of the Fellowship at that time and had brought an agenda for the meeting. As we were about to commence, he said: 'I believe God wants to give us *his* answers to the situations under consideration today, so let's pray.'

We got on our knees and began to seek God's will and

purpose. An hour and a half later, David abruptly said: 'That's it, folks! The meeting's over. I have ticked every item on the agenda, so let's go home!'

When God does it, it's easy. I am not trying to say that there is never any need to discuss or talk through situations, but unless the priority of prayer is uppermost, our solutions will be born out of human reason and not God's wisdom.

When leaders have learned to take everything to the throne of God in prayer, they will then be able to lead their people to do the same.

Abraham did not receive the answer he wanted to his prayer, but he knew that his security lay in trusting God. The story ends with these words: 'When the Lord had finished speaking with Abraham, he left, and Abraham returned home' (Gen 18:33).

Confidence before God gives boldness before men

Self-confidence, a natural human quality, is of doubtful value in terms of spiritual leadership. If you work with human confidence your actions will be confined within its boundaries. When it is strong it will tend towards pride and arrogance; if it is weak it will be ruled by fear.

When you work with the confidence that comes from God, you are acknowledging that human actions cannot produce divine results. You stop dispensing human wisdom and start bringing the wisdom that comes from God. You stop withdrawing through fear and begin to step out in faith. You stop taking credit for the work God does through you and make sure all the glory is given to him.

Surprisingly, people lacking in confidence are putting their trust in their own weak selves and therefore are actually full of self-confidence. Such people find it difficult to acknowledge that this is what they are doing, and consequently fail to put their confidence in God. Paul writes: 'Such confidence as this is ours through Christ before God. Not that we are competent to claim anything for ourselves, but our competence comes from God' (2 Cor 3:4–5).

To stand before God, to listen to his voice, to seek to please him first and foremost, will develop this kind of confidence.

As a leader, you are under constant pressure from many different directions, and you therefore need to guard against becoming trapped at the centre of opposing forces. Paul was conscious of such forces when he wrote: 'Am I now trying to win the approval of men, or of God? Or am I trying to please men? If I were still trying to please men, I would not be a servant of Christ' (Gal 1:10).

If you lead so as to gain people's approval, God will not be pleased and the fruitfulness of your work will be minimal. Leadership that pleases God requires the courage that can only come from him.

Confidence in God comes from understanding his purpose for your life, his purpose for mankind as revealed in the Scriptures, and in particular his purpose for the people who are in your care.

If you really desire that each person should grow into full maturity in Christ, you will have boldness to bring God's word fearlessly into their lives. This does not mean that you will be harsh and abrasive. Thorough reading of Paul's letters clearly shows that the apostle was full of love and compassion. But because of his awareness of the holiness of God, which demands the highest standards, and of the grace of God, which reaches the depth of human need, he was able to lead his people towards 'the measure of the stature of the fulness of Christ' (Eph 4:13 AV).

4

A Man under God's Authority

Surely it should be 'a man *with* authority', not 'a man *under* authority'? The King James translators must have made a mistake. Every time I used to read the story of the healing of the centurion's servant in Matthew 8 the phrase jarred on me and I mentally changed the word. It took many years before I realized that I was wrong, not the translators!

The centurion saw a quality in the ministry of Jesus that he recognized. He saw that when Jesus spoke, there was a greater power operating through him than could be accounted for by mere human influence. He saw beyond Jesus to the power of God. This was not difficult for him to understand, for he was in a similar position with regard to the power of Rome.

When the centurion spoke to the soldiers under his command, they knew that the whole authority of the Roman Empire was behind him. So when he said to Jesus: 'But speak the word only, and my servant shall be healed. For I am a man under authority, having soldiers under me' (Mt 8:8–9 AV), he acknowledged the authority behind Jesus. Jesus responded with astonishment: 'I say unto you, I have not found so great faith, no, not in Israel' (v.10). Jesus had not at that time found anyone who had received an understanding of his authority so simply and clearly. The centurion had seen someone who was subject to a greater authority.

Because Jesus was in submission to that authority, he gained all its power and stature. Jesus himself spoke of this in John 5:19 when he said, 'I tell you the truth, the Son can do nothing by himself; he can do only what he sees his Father doing, because whatever the Father does the Son also does.'

And later on in the same chapter: 'By myself I can do nothing...for I seek not to please myself but him who sent me' (v.30).

Jesus had authority in his ministry because he was in complete submission to his Father. The writer to the Hebrews sums it up like this: 'During the days of Jesus' life on earth, he offered up prayers and petitions with loud cries and tears to the one who could save him from death, and he was heard because of his reverent submission' (Heb 5:7). Only when you are under the authority of God can you exercise the authority of his kingdom.

Authority in practice

I came to understand the importance of this in two different ways. First, through the practical reality of my life in the Bethany Fellowship. I arrived from Cornwall with my wife Joyce and our five children in September 1979, and almost immediately became involved in leadership.

As an elder with Colin Urquhart and David Brown, I soon learned not only what it was to share in leading the Bethany Fellowship, but also what it was to submit my life to two other men. I had not realized how independent I was until I saw what true submission really meant. Not a slavish obedience to one or two others, but a real trusting relationship where we committed ourselves to lives of mutual submission.

To be under God's authority can only have a practical outworking in the context of the body of Christ. I have found that living thus in submission to other men of God and functioning under their authority has been one of the most liberating and enabling things in the whole of my Christian life.

True authority will be recognized by a willingness in others to submit to it. We need to note the difference between authority and authoritarianism. Spiritual authority will glorify God, authoritarianism will merely elevate man. Godly authority will release people into liberty, joy, and fruitfulness; human authoritarianism will bring heaviness and legalism.

Paul said: 'Submit to one another out of reverence for

Christ' (Eph 5:21). Real spiritual authority cannot work unless each person lives in joyful submission. That is why Jesus said: 'The greatest among you should be like the youngest, and the one who rules like the one who serves' (Lk 22:26).

The leader should be the most submitted person in the whole church. Submitted to God, to his word, to his fellow leaders and to the people. Jesus said: 'But I am among you as one who serves' (Lk 22:27).

One way in which I seek to do this is at a meeting we have at home every Sunday night. The whole household meets together and each person submits his or her programme to the others. As each one shares their activities we make adjustments so that if possible we can meet everyone's needs.

Perhaps one afternoon is fixed for a trip to town; lifts are arranged for Coralie's Guides and Craig's part-time job at the Happy Eater. Ben may ask when his school-friend Neil can come to play, and Daniel wants to know when we can all go ten-pin bowling. The adults also submit their activities. The details then go on the calendar and we conclude by praying together and committing our week to God.

This becomes a blueprint for each of us. Therefore if someone wants to book an appointment with me when I have already committed myself to bowling with the family, the priority has been established.

The second way I learnt about being under God's authority came about almost by accident. At the beginning of 1981 we felt we should introduce a training programme for the Fellowship, as we were rapidly growing in numbers and having to respond to ever-increasing demands for ministry. Two parallel courses were arranged: one to deal with personal counselling under David Brown, and another on evangelism that was my responsibility.

As I sat down to prepare, I opened my Bible at Genesis 1. God began to draw my attention to the way he had planned that his creation should live and how it had all been spoiled through man's fall. However, what I found most exciting was the way God guided me to set out what he had shown. Here it is:

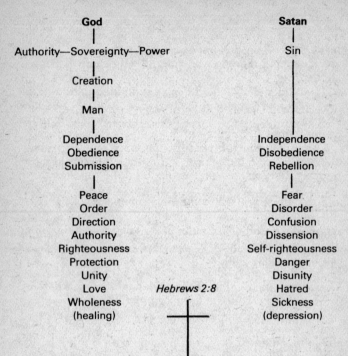

Colossians 1:19–20: For God was pleased to have all his fulness dwell in him, and through him to reconcile to himself all things, whether things on earth or things in heaven, by making peace through his blood, shed on the cross.

The table clearly shows the perfection of God's creation, the effects of man's fall and the significance of the cross in redeeming mankind. It also demonstrates powerfully the whole principle of God's authority and the consequences of operating in independence of him.

I saw how God had brought order and peace into all that he had created. It began with God who had all authority, sovereignty and power. He brought creation into being by his word and the culmination of that creation was man,

42

formed in his own likeness. God gave man dominion because he was under God's authority. Man lived in peace with order in his life in the Garden of Eden, the place of God's providing. There was no sin and so man lived in freedom and perfect righteousness, and was protected from all danger. This combination of factors brought about a situation of unity, love and total wholeness. Until sin entered the picture!

The strategy of the serpent's temptation was to appeal to pride and to precipitate an independent action. 'Did God really say...?' (Gen 3:1). 'Make up your own mind'. 'Do your own thing'. That first sin was not only an act of disobedience, but also one of independence. The result was that Adam and Eve ended up in rebellion against God and had to be banished from the garden.

The consequence for them and for all mankind since has been lives that are dominated by fear, disorder, confusion, dissension, self-righteousness and frustration, to name but a few of the fruits of sin. This has placed man at variance with God and caused him to live with danger, disunity, hatred and sickness as a constant peril.

Praise God that we can be brought back to peace and forgiveness through the death of Jesus. But it is not true to say that the things listed in the right-hand column under Satan disappear the moment we become believers in Christ.

I came to see that when man sinned he came out from under the authority of God and therefore lost his peace, order and protection. It is only when a man turns to God in repentance and faith that he comes back under his covering. I also realized that, even as a Christian, if I fell to the temptation of independence and disobedience, my life could be dominated again by fear and confusion.

This truth was dynamic. I saw the way in which it related not only to my course on evangelism, but to the whole matter of authority. Not only was I working out in practice the benefits of my life being under authority, but I was also understanding how essential it was to live in God's order. I had often heard teaching on how God hated independence and was only content with lives that were lived in complete submission to him. I now grasped that truth for myself.

God's authority brings peace

When our children were very young and there was a violent thunderstorm at night, often one of them would come into our room and climb into bed with Joyce and me. The storm would rage on, but the child would be at peace.

Peace is not the absence of turmoil, but it is to know that God is in control despite the circumstances. Jesus demonstrated that peace throughout his life. He was never hassled. He never manifested worry or anxiety. He could therefore say to his disciples: 'Peace I leave with you; my peace I give you. I do not give to you as the world gives. Do not let your hearts be troubled and do not be afraid' (Jn 14:27). Paul described this as 'the peace of God which transcends all understanding' (Phil 4:7). A peace that is not of human origin is a mark of one under authority. Our strife-torn world is crying out for this quality of peace. However, you will only be able to liberate others into God's peace when you have received it for yourself.

God's authority brings order

There is order in God's creation. The seasons come without faltering, the sun rises and sets in its appointed way. With God's order there is also growth. Seed is sown in its time and the harvest will surely follow. Order is not a dead thing, but a dynamic enabling force.

In the same way, God wants his people to function with order. Leadership exists to bring order into the life and worship of the body of Christ.

In Ephesians 4 we read that the result of the work of apostles, prophets, evangelists, pastors and teachers was 'so that the body of Christ may be built up until we all reach unity in the faith and in the knowledge of the Son of God and become mature, attaining to the whole measure of the fulness of Christ' (vv.12–13).

The questions we may ask concerning people under our care are as follows:

Are they becoming mature in Christ?

Is order coming into their lives?

Do we all have a common purpose?

Is there growth and fruitfulness?

If these things are not happening as they should, it may be because of a lack of authority in the leadership.

'In those days there was no king in Israel: every man did that which was right in his own eyes' (Judg 21:25 AV). That statement could be rewritten for many of today's church situations.

I have even heard some ministers boast of the fact that everyone in their church was happily doing their own thing. It may provide happiness for the people, but it certainly does not result in effectiveness for the kingdom of God. If leadership fails to lead, it will be held responsible for allowing others to act independently and out of harmony with God's purposes.

God's authority brings direction

When Adam and Eve sinned they strayed away from God's direction in their lives. As God's authority is re-established in the lives of his people a clear direction will emerge.

Leadership is needed to convey that direction to the people. Moses received instruction from God as he led the children of Israel out of Egypt and whenever he got stuck he would consult with God who would give him new direction. At times God's instructions were disobeyed, with resulting chaos and hardship. For example, the Israelites, in their early days in Caanan, failed under Joshua's leadership to ask God for wisdom and guidance and so were tricked by the people of Gibeon (Josh 9:14).

Isaiah warned the people against consulting mediums and spiritualists and went on to say, 'Should not a people inquire of their God?' (Is 8:19).

We need direction in our lives, but not the sort that comes from human reasoning or a consensus of opinion. We need

God's direction.

When we live under the authority of God and his word and are in loving, committed relationship, we will be able to hear what God is saying to us. Leaders have the responsibility to bring to the people the direction they have heard from God.

God's authority brings authority

I spent fifteen years of my working life in the family business. It was not an easy thing to come into the company as the boss's son. I had status by accident of birth, but respect needed to be won. As more responsibility was given to me by my father, I was allowed an increasing measure of authority. The more I came under his authority, the more authority I could be given. The staff came to realize that when directions and orders came from me, they had the full backing of my father. I could never have more authority than my father, but I could have as much as he had so long as he was willing to give it to me.

Jesus said: 'All authority in heaven and on earth has been given to me. Therefore go and make disciples of all nations' (Mt 28:18–19). The eleven disciples could be given that authority by Jesus because he had received it from his Father.

True authority cannot come by virtue of position in the church. We can vote anyone into any office we might wish, but true spiritual authority comes from the relationship a man has with God and the degree of his commitment to the body of Christ.

Because Jesus himself has unlimited power, there is no limit to the power he can give to his people. Jesus said: 'Anyone who has faith in me will do what I have been doing. He will do even greater things than these, because I am going to the Father' (Jn 14:12). What an exciting and challenging promise!

You can only pass on a measure of the authority that you have been given. There is no formula or short-cut. The seven sons of Sceva in Acts 19 learned this to their cost. They saw Paul and others releasing people from Satan's power simply by using the name of the Lord Jesus, and thought they would like to have a go. The result was disastrous. The man with the evil spirit jumped on them and overpowered them all, giving them such a beating that they ran out of the house naked and bleeding. His answer to their command was: 'Jesus I know and Paul I know about, but who are you?' (v.25.)

A man under God's authority has access to the resources of heaven and is recognized and feared by all the powers of hell!

God's authority brings righteousness

As we stand in Christ, we are clothed with the righteousness of God. The fact that this is totally unmerited acts as a great leveller in the kingdom of God. Paul put it this way: 'But when the kindness and love of God our Saviour appeared, he saved us, not because of righteous things we had done, but because of his mercy' (Tit 3:4–5).

We cannot take any credit even for being a Christian. We did not do God a good turn when we put our faith in him. And there is nothing we can do now that will gain any merit marks in heaven. It is entirely through God's mercy and grace that we are made righteous. Someone has said, 'Grace is getting what you don't deserve, and mercy is not getting what you do deserve.'

God has given us his righteousness and we have received it by faith. It has placed us in harmony with his holiness and enabled us to be aware of our sinful humanity.

This righteousness comes exclusively from God and there are no righteous deeds I can do that will gain favour with God. It is as Romans 1:17 says: 'a righteousness that is by faith from first to last'. This means that we can confront lost mankind with its unrighteousness not from a position of self-righteousness but because of the grace we have already received from God.

God's authority brings freedom

The words of an ancient prayer say, 'whose service is perfect freedom'. Naturally you would believe that freedom is being able to do what you want to do; however, that level of independence does not in fact produce freedom but makes you a prisoner of your own selfishness.

Children enjoy great freedom when they know the limits within which they can live and play. God's authority brings you within the boundaries of his will and when you operate within those boundaries you will enjoy great freedom. In Psalm 40:8 we read: 'I desire to do your will, O my God; your law is within my heart.'

Adam and Eve enjoyed the freedom of the garden of Eden as long as they remained under God's authority. But after the Fall they lost their freedom and became slaves to sin.

Frustration occurs in leadership when human desire conflicts with the ways of God. This may happen because the people want their own way and not God's way, which will require courage to confront. It can also happen because a leader is motivated by selfish ambition instead of submission to the purposes of God.

God's authority brings protection

One of the differences between true authority and authoritarianism is that the former provides protection for those under its care, whereas the latter seeks only to protect itself.

When a husband takes his rightful place as leader in the home, he provides protection for his wife and children. It is interesting how Paul uses the example of the husband/wife relationship when he is showing how Christ cares for his church:

> Husbands, love your wives, just as Christ loved the church and gave himself up for her to make her holy, cleansing her by the washing with water through the word, and to present her to himself as a radiant church, without stain or wrinkle or any other blemish, but holy and blameless (Eph 5:25–27).

Our first home had four staircases. When our children reached the crawling stage of their development we were faced with a problem. Could we make all those staircases safe so as to prevent the children from falling down them? That was not realistic, as part of our home was used for our youth fellowship and a large number of people were continually using it. The solution was to teach the children how not to fall downstairs. As each one crawled to the brink of danger, we would turn them around and teach them how to slide down backwards on their tummies. There were a few tumbles, but the lesson was quickly learnt. The children's submission to our authority was vital for their safety and protection. They are all alive and well now, so it must have worked!

The family of God should be a place of caring and protection. The Bethany Fellowship of which I am a part has a community lifestyle, which we believe to be in line with the teachings of Scripture. The psalmist says: 'A father to the fatherless, a defender of widows, is God in his holy dwelling. God sets the lonely in families, he leads forth the prisoners with singing' (Ps 68:5–6).

This does not mean a vast number of people crammed into a large house. The focus is on family and we live in extended households where single people become part of a family that is centred upon a married couple and their children. We believe that every person in the body needs leadership, provision and protection and this is the intention of our community households.

A description in the book of Acts of life in the early church contains this challenging statement: 'There were no needy persons among them' (Acts 4:34).

God's authority brings unity

'My prayer is not for them alone. I pray also for those who will believe in me through their message, that all of them may be one, Father, just as you are in me and I am in you' (Jn 17:20–21).

We can know unity in the church if we will simply follow the teachings of Jesus and some basic scriptural principles. First, God calls his people together to be an expression of his body in the place where he has put them. Secondly, God raises up leaders among them to hear his voice and to direct his people. Thirdly, principles of truth and life are given to the body of Christ to guide it into growth and fruitfulness.

However, there are no rigid rules that are going to guarantee success. As we acknowledge our need—that we deserve nothing but God's judgement—and reach out to receive his mercy and forgiveness, so we are made one in him. This is a position both of humility and of privilege. 'God opposes the proud but gives grace to the humble' (Jas 4:6).

Unity begins with hearts that meet at the cross of Jesus. Unity grows as hearts are bound together in loving relationship. Unity gathers strength as leaders commit themselves to one another and listen to God's direction together. 'Submit to one another out of reverence for Christ' (Eph 5:21). The outcome of unity is God's blessing: 'For there the Lord bestows his blessing, even life for evermore' (Ps 133:3).

Why then is there so much disunity? Part of the problem is that men seek oneness of mind and belief without establishing fusion of hearts. The Christian church has been left a legacy of division from ages past, but this does not mean that it is impossible for God's people to live in harmony now.

We have a choice: we can argue that because of all the failure of history we are justified in living in disunity today; or we can receive the promises of God and work out the reality of actually living in unity today. It all stems from a living relationship with God and a loving commitment to Christ's body.

I live in unity with my wife Joyce. That does not mean that we always agree about everything, but because our love and commitment are so deep we work through our difficulties and make sure we arrive at harmonious solutions. So it should be with God's people.

God's authority brings love

A real quality of love will be seen among a people who submit to God's authority. The sure knowledge of God's love and the extent of his mercy give birth to a caring, sacrificial love among his people. Jesus summed it up beautifully when he explained to the Pharisees why a sinful woman had anointed him with expensive perfume: 'Therefore, I tell you, her many sins have been forgiven—for she loved much. But he who has been forgiven little loves little' (Lk 7:47).

Security that stems from loving and being loved should be a hallmark of the family of God. The church is made up of forgiven sinners who are bound together in God's love. Sadly, there is often a lack of love in the church today, because we have tried to separate love for God from love for people.

John writes about this in his first letter: 'We love because he first loved us. If anyone says, 'I love God,' yet hates his brother, he is a liar. For anyone who does not love his brother, whom he has seen, cannot love God, whom he has not seen' (1 Jn 4:19–20). These are strong words and need to be a continual challenge to all of us. To be obedient means to live constantly in forgiveness and openness with brothers and sisters in Christ. This rules out all bitterness, division and hatred. The more we understand of the great love God has shown us, and the more we know of his forgiveness for us, the more we will be able to live in love and forgiveness towards others.

God's authority brings healing

Healing of body, mind and spirit is intrinsic to the kingdom of God. To leave out physical healing is to limit God's power, but it is also a mistake to place such a strong emphasis on healing of the body that the full breadth of God's restorative power is lost. The healing of Jesus leads to wholeness and discipleship. It needs to be an integral part of local church life so that the family of God can live in the wholeness of God.

When Jesus healed the ten lepers, only one returned to give thanks to him. 'One of them, when he saw he was healed, came back, praising God in a loud voice. He threw himself at Jesus' feet and thanked him—and he was a Samaritan. Jesus asked, "Were not all ten cleansed? Where are the other nine? Was no-one found to return and give praise to God except this foreigner?" Then he said to him, "Rise and go; your faith has made you well [whole AV]' (Lk 17:15–19). All ten were healed, but only one was made whole. Healing that does not lead to discipleship does not bring wholeness.

To live under God's authority is to enjoy great blessing, security and fruitfulness. It is the only basis for effective leadership in the body of Christ.

5

A Man Who Lives in Revival

'My faith for these missions is that you leave revival behind you. But you do not have that faith.'

That was the message God gave to Colin Urquhart and the team in 1981 as we prepared for a summer of week-long missions in various towns in the United Kingdom, starting at Southport, Merseyside.

God was right! He wanted to bring revival to Southport, but that was totally beyond our faith and expectations.

Revival in the sense of those great movements of the Holy Spirit that sweep through whole communities (in the Hebrides and Cornwall in the past, in East Africa and the Philippines today) is a sovereign work of God. Revival on a personal level comes when we respond totally to God. We cannot bring revival about; God alone does that, but our individual disobedience and unbelief can delay or even prevent him from acting.

At Southport, the realization of our personal responsibility in the matter led to a wholehearted seeking after God in his revival power. (Colin has written in detail about this time in chapters 13 and 14 of his book *Faith for the Future* (Hodder & Stoughton 1982).)

It was for me a most significant time of growth, and that particular day at Southport was like the first flicker of light that comes before dawn. 'It *is* possible to experience personal revival,' I realized. 'I *can* meet with God in such a way that his revival power can flow through me.'

The revelation was exciting yet daunting. I knew it was said of Jesus: 'And he did not do many miracles there [in Nazareth] because of their lack of faith' (Mt 13:58). I became aware of my lack of faith and the way that my life had limited God. There was no sense of despair about this, but I longed for God to deal with me.

As we returned home, we began to read some of the books that had come out of revival situations. There was *Finney on Revival* by Charles Finney (E. E. Shelhamer (ed.), Dimension Books, Bethany Fellowship Inc.) and *The Calvary Road* by Roy Hession (CLC). Roy Hession had a simple definition of revival: 'Revival is just the life of the Lord Jesus poured into human hearts.' I was beginning to understand: 'Revival places God in his right place and it puts me in my right place.'

Revival brings conviction of sin and brokenness

It was Easter 1981 and most of the community were going away for a short break. As we met for our final prayer time, Colin came in with a sheaf of papers in his hand and gave us each a copy. It was a list of factors that prevent or hinder revival and was entitled 'Preparing for Revival'. It had been condensed from Finney's book. The list was intimidating: examine your heart concerning—wrong relationships and attitudes towards others; dissension towards those in authority; jealousy; speaking evil of others; worldliness; secret sins; laxity in spiritual discipline; unreliability; hardness of heart (especially towards God's word); unholiness; lack of openness towards others...

The list continued with further hindrances: a lack of gratitude and love towards God; neglect of the Bible, prayer, family responsibilities, watchfulness over oneself and one's brethren; neglect of self-denial and the means of grace. Other stumbling blocks were unbelief; pride; envy; slander; levity; lying; cheating; hypocrisy; robbing God; bad temper; and hindering others from being useful.

Now we knew why we had not experienced revival. Off we went to search our hearts and come to God in repentance. We were not being crushed by condemnation, but being liberated as we allowed God to expose our lives to a new depth.

The following day I set off with the family for Scotland, to an isolated croft in the Western Highlands. We were taking a week's break with our children. This was also a significant time of meeting with God. Each morning Joyce and I arose early, made a cup of coffee and went out to the cliff top to pray.

As the sun rose and shed its early morning light on the Isle of Skye and the Cuillins we worked our way steadily through the list, a few things each day. We did not set out to expose one another's sin, but concentrated on our own. Each spoke out the things that God was saying and then prayed them through.

It was one of the loveliest holidays we have ever had. We were blessed with six days of sunshine which aided our relaxation and fun, and with God at work in the way he was it also became the holiest holiday we have ever spent!

I now clearly understood that revival does not fall out of the sky like a bolt of lightning, but comes to those who are seriously seeking God and are prepared to be dealt with by him. Later I was to read accounts of past revivals and discovered that at the centre of every sovereign awakening of God were people who were resolutely seeking him.

The initial preparation for revival is to allow God to reveal sin in your life by his Holy Spirit. Conviction of sin should then lead to confession. That is what was happening on the cliff top in Scotland. God was putting his finger on one area after another in our lives and we were confessing to God and to one another.

We began to understand in a new way the truth of the words: 'Therefore confess your sins to each other and pray for each other so that you may be healed' (Jas 5:16). That brought a new depth of understanding into our marriage and released the cleansing of God into our lives. As John writes: 'If we confess our sins, he is faithful and just and will forgive us our sins and purify us from all unrighteousness' (1 Jn 1:9). As God meets with you in his holiness there will always be conviction, confession and cleansing. That is the preparation.

But true revival goes deeper than that. Conviction needs to lead to repentance. Repentance precedes brokenness and

55

radical change. It is possible to confess the same sin over and over again. Each time God is faithful and you will receive forgiveness and cleansing, but saying 'sorry' is not repentance. Repentance involves not only confession with regard to sin, but a change of will which is expressed in altered behaviour. Your will is thus set in line with God's will.

Charles Finney writes in *True and False Repentance* (Kregel Publications, 1966):

> If you have truly repented, you do not now love sin; you do not now abstain from it through fear, and to avoid punishment, but because you hate it. How is this with you? Do you know that your disposition to commit sin is gone? Look at the sins you used to practice when you were impenitent—how do they appear to you? Do they look pleasant—and would you really love to practice them again if you dared? If you do, if you have the disposition to sin left, you are only convicted. Your *opinions* of sin may be changed, but if the love of that sin remains, as your soul lives, you are still an impenitent sinner.

True repentance leads to brokenness. Brokenness is a word that is much misunderstood. Many people think that it is to be so demoralized before God that you collapse in a heap of discouragement. What a lie of the enemy! Brokenness deals with your selfishness and pride so that the life of Jesus is liberated within you.

Roy Hession put it like this in *The Calvary Road*:

> To be broken is the beginning of revival. It is painful, it is humiliating, but it is the only way. It is being 'not *I*, but *Christ*', and a 'C' is a bent 'I'. The Lord Jesus cannot live in us fully and reveal Himself through us until the proud self within us is broken. This simply means that the hard, unyielding self, which justifies itself, wants its own way, stands up for its rights, and seeks its own glory, at last bows its head to God's will, admits its wrong, gives up its own way to Jesus, surrenders its rights, and discards its own glory—that the Lord Jesus might have all and be all. In other words, it is dying to self and self-attitudes.

Revival leads to holiness

As we gathered again after the Easter holiday, it was clear
that God had been at work in significant ways. Repentance
had brought a new release of the Spirit's power. But some of
us were far from satisfied.

We knew that there must be something more to revival
than we had yet experienced. Colin began to teach about
holiness at our daily morning prayer times. It is amazing
how we had overlooked the scriptural teaching about holiness.
During recent years there has been much teaching on the
Holy Spirit and the need for more power, love and joy, but
who wants to be holy?

'Make every effort to live in peace with all men and to be
holy; without holiness no-one will see the Lord' (Heb 12:14).

'But just as he who called you is holy, so be holy in all you
do; for it is written: "Be holy, because I am holy"' (1 Pet
1:15–16).

God desires a holy people who are set apart for him. How
can it happen? Is it really possible?

The first Monday of May that year was a Bank Holiday
and we were all looking forward to a long weekend with our
families. As some of us were praying together on the Friday
lunchtime, God made it clear that we were to abandon our
plans and devote the whole weekend to seeking him. Saturday
was to be a day of prayer and all the adults in the community
were to gather in the evening.

As we came together, Colin introduced the meeting by
saying: 'I have never been here before and haven't any idea
what is going to happen. We have come to meet with God, so
let's pray.' This was followed by a simple one-sentence
prayer: 'Lord, please come and meet with us in your holiness.'

We began with worship. It was different—not the joyful
praise that often happens at the beginning of a meeting, but
praise with a depth and beauty that was new. There was a
word of prophecy. But the most powerful aspect of the
meeting was the sense that Jesus was among us in his holiness.
His holiness was revealing our unholiness and we began to
cry out to the Lord for his forgiveness and mercy. Spon-

taneously there was open confession of sin. To pray sitting down became totally inappropriate so we fell to our knees and on our faces before God. There was deep conviction and tears. Much of the confession was concerning relationships: forgiveness and reconciliation was happening all around. Time stood still as God brought us through repentance to his peace.

We had just begun to understand those words of David: 'Create in me a pure heart, O God, and renew a steadfast spirit within me' (Ps 51:10).

We sought the Lord again on the Sunday and Monday evenings and each time God took us deeper. More of the darkness of our hearts was brought into the light and dealt with.

As Monday evening was drawing to a close, we had a tremendous sense of the glory of God among us. We rose to our feet to shout our praises to him who had so graciously revealed himself to us.

I have since pondered the way God dealt with us at that time, to see what principles were involved. It seems there were three components to God's work among us.

First, there was what Finney would call 'breaking up the fallow ground'. That began with the paper headed 'Preparing for Revival', which the Fellowship has now nicknamed 'The Finney Repentance List'! Deliberate and thorough repentance is a vital prelude to revival.

Secondly, there was anointed teaching from God's word. It covered many areas including holiness and the renewing of our minds. It produced more repentance and was very fruitful.

But thirdly, there was the May weekend when the repentance lists and the teaching were laid aside and we came together in the presence of God. God by his Spirit was able to uncover things that would never have been revealed through Finney's list and the teaching alone. But time had to be found, even if it cost us a much needed weekend break, in which we made sure we really did seek the Lord's face in a new way.

This is the reason why all three components are at the heart of The Hyde Leaders' Weeks. There is teaching from the word, time is given for searching hearts with the Finney list, but most important is the time spent with God in his holiness. All these things can be done alone with God, but it is a great blessing to seek God with others who have the same desire.

Revival releases God's light into your life

No one told us that when God revealed himself to us in his holiness we would find ourselves confessing our sins to each other. We later read that it was a feature of revivals throughout history. If we had known this, some of us may not have been so eager to meet with him! Why does this happen?

It is because God is light and when invited to come among his people, he not only comes as the holy God but also as the light. His light exposes the darkness of our hearts. 'But if we walk in the light, as he is in the light, we have fellowship with one another, and the blood of Jesus, his Son, purifies us from every sin' (1 Jn 1:7).

It is in his presence that darkness is exposed and our hearts cry out in confession and repentance. True fellowship with God is marred if there is the darkness of unconfessed sin. Fear of open confession disappears when the reality of God is greater than the awareness of the people around. It becomes more important to know that I am right with God than that my reputation is preserved before men.

That darkness will not only have spoilt my fellowship with God, but will have affected my relationships with my Christian brother or sister. So, I will want to confess that sin to the one who has been hurt by it and receive forgiveness. This is what it means to 'walk in the light'.

There are three elements to walking in the light. First, it is towards God. When the light of God's holiness shines into my life and exposes the darkness, my first concern is to get right with God. Therefore, I confess my sin to God and receive his cleansing according to the promise of 1 John 1:9. Walking in the light produces cleansing.

Secondly, it is towards others. Sin is never private. It will always affect others either directly or indirectly, so I need to confess my sin to the ones who have been touched by it. That is the James 5:16 principle: 'Therefore confess your sins to each other and pray for each other so that you may be healed.' Walking in the light produces healing of relationships, hurts and misunderstanding; reconciliation where sin has divided; restoration where sin has caused alienation.

Thirdly, it defeats Satan. Confession with the mouth is very powerful. Let me explain by giving a personal example.

In the middle of all that God was doing during the summer of 1981, I suddenly discovered that one of the girls in the team was having an effect on me that was both disturbing and difficult to understand. It did not seem to have arisen out of my action or hers. Nothing overt was happening between us. My marriage was under no strain and my love for Joyce was continuing to grow and become stronger rather than weaker. No, this seemed to be an attack from the enemy who was trying to bring darkness into my life and to promote sin.

I was puzzling over this, having prayed about it, when it occurred to me that I should have a chat with David Brown, one of my fellow elders. I went to see him in his study one morning and told him the situation, looking for his help. He simply said: 'Now you have walked in the light with me about this you don't need to worry any more. The enemy's power is broken.' He was right. I walked out of that room a free man. I saw a new depth of meaning in Romans 10:10— 'For it is with your heart that you believe and are justified, and it is with your mouth that you confess and are saved.' Walking in the light produces victory over temptation and sin; however, just a word of warning—open confession that is too detailed and intimate can do more harm than good. For example, to confess lustful thoughts will cause no problem if described simply by those two words, but any more detail would be harmful to the hearers and would not release any more healing into the life of the person making the confession.

As with the situation just recounted, when the situation is delicate, walk in the light simply with one other person.

These principles are particularly important for those who are called to be leaders. The pressure and the potential isolation of leadership produces extreme vulnerability. It is sad to hear of the number of people whose lives and ministries are being destroyed through moral lapses and other areas of sin that need never have happened had they walked in the light with just one other person.

One of the results of revival is that it liberates the power of God into your life and ministry in new ways. It also activates the enemy to attack with ever greater ferocity. You need to have every spiritual weapon sharp and ready for use.

It is important that a leader is really open and ready to walk in the light with others. Your openness will release openness in others. As you make walking in the light a principle of your life, those you lead will quickly follow—that is, if they are serious about God and want to live in his revival power.

Revival produces powerful prayer

On the Tuesday that followed the weekend of meeting with God, we were up early and set out for Grimsby where we were to hold a pre-mission rally. Even as we drove up the motorway we realized that something was different. Normally we would chat, listen to some praise cassettes or perhaps some teaching. This time, all we wanted to do was to pray and worship the Lord.

When we arrived at the Ice House and set up all the equipment, we were planning our time so as to leave the normal half hour of prayer before the start of the meeting. We now found this to be totally inadequate and had to reschedule our daily timetable so as to have two hours of prayer before each meeting.

These times were not simply for praying about the meeting, but revival prayer in the presence of God when he could liberate his power in and through us. That which had characterized the revival weekend continued. Open confession of sin came naturally and quickly. There was a tremendous sense of God's peace and we were constantly aware of his holy presence among us. There was a new release of faith for the ministry and a fresh concern for the lost.

The whole subject of prayer will be more fully dealt with in a later chapter. However, it is important to understand that prevailing prayer is a vital ingredient of true revival. Too much of our praying is given to asking God to do things in others and not enough to seeking God to do things in us.

Charles Finney writes about moving God in prayer in *Revivals of Religion* (Morgan & Scott, 1835):

> When I speak of moving God, I do not mean that God's mind is changed by prayer, or that his disposition or character is changed. But prayer produces such a change *in us* as renders it consistent for God to do as it would not be consistent for him to do otherwise. When a sinner repents, that state of feeling makes it proper for God to forgive him. God has always been ready to forgive him on that condition, so that when the sinner changes his feelings and repents, it requires no change of feeling in God to pardon him. It is the sinner's repentance that renders his forgiveness proper, and is the occasion of God's acting as he does. So when Christians offer effectual prayer, their state of feeling renders it proper for God to answer them.

That weekend of seeking God transformed the whole character of the Fellowship's prayer life. The true essence of revival brings a new awareness of the greatness of God and the utter futility of human endeavour. It ends the kind of prayer that says 'God bless what I am doing for you.' Instead, it starts the kind of prayer that cries out for God to move in his sovereignty and power; and thoroughly humbles God's people as they realize that he chooses to pour out his power and might through human instruments such as themselves.

Revival liberates love and unity

There is nothing like a good dose of the glory of God to sort out bickering and disunity. Our meeting with God in the community brought us through to a new depth of love and oneness.

When we try to sort out our differences by means of discussion and argument, we will often end up with our opinions more fixed and our positions more deeply entrenched than ever. When we bring our varied viewpoints before the throne of God we will hear his voice and that brings us all to repentance and unity.

We have a phrase in the Bethany Fellowship that is used of a situation that has become gritty and generally unfruitful: 'What we need there is a bit of revival'. What does this mean?

Several months ago during a Leaders' Week it became obvious to me that there was a certain amount of bad feeling among the people who live at The Hyde and among the team who work with me on these Weeks. Much of this was justified as there had been thoughtlessness and neglect in some areas. Rather than call a meeting to sort it all out, I suggested a day of prayer and fasting. When we were all together I simply said: 'A lot of things went wrong last week which were not helpful or glorifying to the Lord. I am not really interested in who was right or who was wrong. I believe that what we need is to find the Lord together. Let's worship God and seek him.'

An hour and a half later peace had been restored, we had walked in the light and, in addition, suggestions had come during the prayer which solved many of the problems that had previously seemed insurmountable. Why? Because we had met with God.

Let me add that I am not advocating revival prayer as a cure for bad organization or mismanagement. God requires that we should be good stewards and faithful in all we are given to do. But even in the best ordered circles there is the need for the revival prayer that keeps love and unity alive and fresh.

Revival results in a hunger for God which leads to more revival

'The Lord is near to all who call on him,' writes David in Psalm 145:18. When you meet with God in his revival power you get to know him better. The more you know of God the more you want to know. Your heart responds with agreement to the words of the psalmist: 'My heart and my flesh cry out for the living God' (Ps 84:2).

Even in the face of this deep desire within to know more of

God, there is still temptation and failure, and it is all too easy to fall away from that level of spiritual vitality.

After an intense summer of mission in 1981 we devoted most of August to having holidays with our families. The first thing we were aware of on our return was that we had slipped back from the place of revival in which we had been living several weeks earlier. So as soon as possible a day was set aside to meet with God afresh and allow him to work again in each of us.

How does revival affect leadership?

A leader must first meet with God in his revival power and through brokenness find the repentance that leads him to the foot of the cross to receive cleansing and experience a fresh anointing of God's power through his Holy Spirit. God is then in his rightful place at the centre of the leader's life and work, and the leader is in his right place before God. Revival is an antidote to pride in leadership, and releases prayer and faith in the people.

In revival, God shows you his view of your sin—and leads you to repentance.

In revival, God shows you his view of your life—and leads you to holiness.

In revival, God shows you his view of other Christians—and leads you into new relationships of love and living in the light with one another.

In revival, God shows you his view of the world—and leads you into a new heart compassion for the lost.

Does this then mean that when God sends a mighty spiritual awakening through the nation (as he did in Wesley's day) that it will necessarily be through those who are actively seeking his revival power? It may be, or it may not: God is sovereign. But it is certainly true that God's revived people are instruments he can use to promote such an awakening, and equally true that his people's disobedience and unbelief can delay or even prevent revival.

I can identify with many things that have happened in past revivals, but there are other manifestations of God's power that I have not yet seen. I long to see God move in Holy Spirit fire in this land as he did in bygone days.

I will conclude this chapter with a quotation from Richard Owen Roberts's book on *Revival* (Tyndale, 1982) which beautifully sums up that longing for a greater outpouring of revival:

When can revival be expected? If revival is the extraordinary movement of the Holy Spirit, it can be expected when the sovereign God of the universe sends it. And when is God likely to send an extraordinary work? At a time of extraordinary need when his people are in the grip of an extraordinary desire and when nothing short of an extraordinary outpouring of the Holy Spirit will satisfy.

6

A Man Who Lives at the Cross

The cross is a symbol of death. It stands for the abrupt, violent
end of a human being. The man in Roman times who took up his
cross and started down the road had already said goodbye to his
friends. He was not coming back. He was going out to have it
ended. The cross made no compromise, modified nothing, spared
nothing; it slew all of the man, completely and for good. It did not
try to keep on good terms with its victim. It struck cruelly and
hard, and when it had finished its work, the man was no more.

God salvages the individual by liquidating him and then
raising him again to newness of life.

In coming to Christ we do not bring our old life up onto a
higher plane; we leave it at the cross. The corn of wheat must fall
into the ground and die (A. W. Tozer, *The Alliance Witness*, 1946).

The cross of Christ is the most revolutionary thing to have
appeared among men. However, unless the cross stands at
the centre of the life and ministry of a leader, other things will
compete for pre-eminence. That is why Paul says: 'But God
forbid that I should glory, save in the cross of our Lord Jesus
Christ, by whom the world is crucified unto me, and I unto
the world' (Gal 6:14 av).

Colin had been invited by Noel Proctor, chaplain at
Strangeways Prison, Manchester, to preach at the Sunday
morning service. The five hundred or so prisoners had filed
into the church, hymns had been sung and the opening
prayers prayed. Colin was introduced and he walked forward
to preach. 'I have good news for you all today,' he said. 'God
does not want to reform you!' A ripple of laughter spread
through the gathered company. Colin continued: 'No, God
does not want to reform you. He wants you to die.' The

stunned silence that followed guaranteed an attentive hearing as Colin declared the power of the cross to pronounce death to the old life and to usher in the new life in Christ.

The cross is the place of forgiveness

Sin is an unpopular word in today's world. Only the most serious crimes against society or the gravest moral lapses are labelled sin. This leads many respectable church-going people to feel that their lifestyle is acceptable to God. If sin is minimized on the one hand, the power of the cross will be diminished on the other.

Sin is described very simply in the Bible: 'We all, like sheep, have gone astray, each of us has turned to his own way' (Is 53:6). What is sin? In simple terms it is going our own way rather than God's way. What then about our good deeds? The response of Scripture is: 'all our righteous acts are like filthy rags' (Is 64:6).

We have all sinned and fallen short of God's holiness and righteousness, therefore we all need to receive the work of the cross as our only way to salvation and forgiveness. There is nothing we can do to merit God's mercy. He gives it to us freely by his grace through the death of Jesus. As Paul says to the Ephesians: 'In him we have redemption through his blood, the forgiveness of sins, in accordance with the riches of God's grace' (Eph 1:7).

As those called to leadership, let us never forget the wonder of the free gift of forgiveness that we have in Jesus. As a bumper sticker seen in America put it: 'We Christians aren't perfect—just forgiven!'

The cross is the place of victory over sin

In *Pilgrim's Progress* there is a picture of Pilgrim climbing up the hill to the cross with a heavy load of sin on his back. As he arrives at the cross and receives forgiveness, the load falls off and rolls away never to be seen again.

The cross is certainly the place where we receive forgiveness of sins and where we enter new life in Christ. But it is possible to confine the cross in our thinking and experience to being a place of forgiveness alone and not realize the breadth of Christ's sacrifice for us on Calvary.

The extraordinary truth is that when Jesus died he took my sins to death with him and he also took *me*, all of me: 'I have been crucified with Christ and I no longer live, but Christ lives in me' (Gal 2:20). My self-life has been annihilated with Jesus: 'So you also must consider yourselves dead to sin and alive to God in Christ Jesus' (Rom 6:11 RSV).

Not only has the work of the cross achieved forgiveness for sins committed, but it has also won victory over sin itself. The resurrection of Jesus pronounced victory over death and it also declared triumph over the power of sin in fallen humanity. That means that you do not have to remain a slave to sin, disobedience or bad habits.

Even though you have the assurance of sins forgiven, you can often remain in slavery to temptation. Does that mean that you are to spend the rest of your life in an unequal struggle with sin? Certainly not. Paul is writing to Christians when he says: 'Put to death, therefore, whatever belongs to your earthly nature: sexual immorality, impurity, lust, evil desires and greed, which is idolatry' (Col 3:5). You *can* live in victory over temptation and sin!

Paul says to the Romans: 'For we know that our old self was crucified with him so that the body of sin might be rendered powerless, that we should no longer be slaves to sin—because anyone who has died has been freed from sin' (Rom 6:6–7).

For years the cross was for me no more than the place where my sins were forgiven. I never understood that I could know victory over the power of sin through the cross, and so I lived in defeat and powerlessness. You see, I have more problems with myself than I do with my sin! I knew my sins were forgiven, but I thought that I would have to wait until I was in heaven before I could know victory over my human weakness. When the light came I was thrilled to know that whatever sin may try to drag me down there is victory for me *now!* I do not have to wait until beyond the grave.

How do you receive this victory? First, recognize those

areas of darkness, failure and compromise as sin. Ask God to show you the evil of your sin and to enable you to truly repent—that is, to turn away from it. Bring what he has shown you to the cross and ask God for his forgiveness and cleansing.

Confess in the presence of another Christian: 'Therefore confess your sins to each other and pray for each other so that you may be healed' (Jas 5:16). That brings the darkness into God's light and breaks the power of it in your life, as I explained more fully in the last chapter.

The greater your leadership responsibility, the greater will be the pressures on your life, and it will be increasingly important for you to know the daily reality of victory over personal sin. You will then be able to lead others into the knowledge of how to live in victory over sin.

Jesus lived a victorious life, and through the cross he provided the way for us to follow in his steps. 'For we do not have a high priest who is unable to sympathise with our weaknesses, but we have one who has been tempted in every way, just as we are—yet was without sin' (Heb 4:15).

The cross is the place of victory over Satan

In considering the work of Satan in our lives and churches we find two extremes of belief, both of which need to be guarded against. On the one hand there are some who deny the very existence of Satan, and on the other there are those who blame him for every negative influence. To deny his existence is to give him room to operate freely and unhindered. To blame him for everything that goes wrong is to attribute to him far more influence than he deserves and to create fear among the people.

It is true that Satan encourages sin and disobedience. But to blame him for all ills removes from individuals their responsibility for their own sin and wrongdoing and masks the real root of the trouble.

Satan is real and powerful and it is important to recognize with Paul that: 'our struggle is not against flesh and blood, but against the rulers, against the authorities, against the powers of this dark world and against the spiritual forces of evil in the heavenly realms' (Eph 6:12).

Satan's forces are at work in the world today. Missionaries who have worked in primitive countries have been conscious of demon powers for years. We might be tempted to think that in the civilized West these forces do not exist. That is not so. We need to be aware of the powers of darkness at work in our land today. But we need to balance that fact with the knowledge that Satan and all his forces were utterly defeated at the cross. And they know it!

A minister, let me call him Graham, who came on a recent Leaders' Week had been going through a time of great darkness and arrived at The Hyde in some considerable distress. As I observed him during a time of prayer I could see that he was struggling. At the coffee break I sat down beside him. 'What needs to happen to you?' I asked. 'I need to be set free from all that has been attacking me,' he replied. We agreed a time when we could meet.

It is important when confronting the powers of darkness not to minister alone, so Francis, a member of my team, joined me and the three of us met for prayer. Graham explained how Satan had been oppressing him and causing great depression and weakness; there had even been a time during the night when he had experienced something near to physical strangulation. An attempt had been made to release him which had caused him to vomit and become violent.

I told him that it was not going to happen this time. We prayed and took authority in the name of Jesus. However, the moment we started to pray for his release Graham started to choke and retch. I immediately looked at him, but addressed the powers of darkness. 'You can stop that in the name of Jesus,' I commanded. Even as we continued to minister there were other manifestations that were firmly rebuked in the name of the Lord. I knew that through the cross there was total victory and I was not prepared to accept anything less.

In a short while Graham prayed a beautiful prayer of repentance and was set free from all that oppressed him. The whole room was bathed in peace as we reached the place of victory. 'I feel as though a light has been turned on,' he said, as he basked in the freedom and joy that God had given him.

Satan has been robbed of his power and knows that his final sentence has already been pronounced and will most surely be carried out. Paul reminds us of this in Colossians 2:15: 'And having disarmed the powers and authorities, he made a public spectacle of them, triumphing over them by the cross.

God's word gives us the assurance that any evidence of the activity of Satan in the life of someone we meet need not be a cause for fear, for we know that through the triumph of the cross we have the right to victory.

It is not my purpose here to explore the whole subject of spiritual warfare, as there are many books that cover this subject. (My recommendation would be *Spiritual Warfare* by Michael Harper, reissued by Kingsway Publications, 1983.) But I wish to make clear that we need to declare the fact that the cross has dealt completely with all the powers of darkness. This means that we do not have to make excuses for defeat, failure or any activity of Satan in our lives, but we can always know victory through the cross. 'This is the victory that has overcome the world, even our faith. Who is it that overcomes the world? Only he who believes that Jesus is the Son of God' (1 Jn 5:4–5).

The cross is the place of victory over sickness

When sin entered the world it not only brought judgement on mankind because of disobedience towards God, but it also brought decay and sickness upon the human body.

The cross is where sin, death and sickness have been thoroughly dealt with. Sin is cleansed in the blood of Jesus. Death has been destroyed: 'Where, O death, is your victory? Where, O death, is your sting?' (1 Cor 15:55). 'Christ Jesus …has destroyed death and has brought life and immortality to light through the gospel' (2 Tim 1:10).

Sickness has been defeated through the death of Jesus. In 1 Peter 2:24 we read, 'By his wounds you have been healed.' We need to understand here that all the suffering Jesus experienced leading up to his death upon the cross was part of God's plan of redemption. God would not have allowed unnecessary pain to his dearly loved Son. So beginning with the suffering in the Garden of Gethsemane where the agony caused him to sweat drops of blood, the flogging he received through Pilate, the crown of thorns, the wounds of the nails of crucifixion right through to the sword that pierced his side after he had died—all this was a necessary part of God's purpose. Even when Jesus cried out: 'My God, my God, why have you forsaken me?' he was experiencing an alienation that would make way for his healing power to reach to the depths of human rejection and suffering.

Peter and John demonstrated the reality of God's healing grace when the man was cured of his lameness at the temple gate called Beautiful. When asked by the rulers and elders for an explanation, Peter boldly declared: 'It is by the name of Jesus Christ of Nazareth, whom you crucified but whom God raised from the dead, that this man stands before you completely healed' (Acts 4:10).

We can see that it is clearly God's purpose that healing and wholeness should be an intrinsic part of the gospel. Healing is in the atonement. We realize that when God forgives our sins he gives us eternal life—his own holy life. Because of its eternal quality it can never die and is therefore everlasting. When we are healed physically or emotionally God is glorified, the works of darkness are defeated and we are participating in the wholeness of Jesus.

However, our mortal bodies are still subject to decay and will not escape natural death (unless Jesus returns again first). That is why Paul says: 'flesh and blood cannot inherit the kingdom of God, nor does the perishable inherit the imperishable' (1 Cor 15:50). Natural death is not a tragedy for a Christian, but the gateway to the fullness of all that God has provided for us through the death and resurrection of Jesus.

It is not my intention to explore the whole subject of healing, but to show that when we grasp the totality of the work of the cross we can confidently minister the wholeness of Jesus to spirit, mind and body.

The cross is the pathway to power

During recent years there has been a great emphasis on the need to be filled with the Holy Spirit so that more of God's life and power can be released into hearts and lives. This is good and right and the teaching of Scripture. Why, then, among those who have been filled with the Holy Spirit, do some people manifest God's power so much more than others? Has anyone stopped to ask how much is being filled? God cannot take up his rule and reign where humanity and sin reign. We must willingly give over each area of our life to God's control. A. W. Tozer has said:

> It may be said without qualification that every man is as holy and as full of the Spirit as he wants to be. He may not be as full as he wishes he were, but he is most certainly as full as he wants to be.

The cross is therefore the pathway to power because it is only as the death of Jesus is at work in our lives, dealing with our sinful humanity, that God is able to fill us more fully with his life and power.

You can be crying out to God for more of his Holy Spirit and wonder why your life remains unaffected. What you need is more of the cross. Here again is the message of Romans 6—not only to be dead to sin but to be alive to God in Christ Jesus: 'Therefore do not let sin reign in your mortal body so that you obey its evil desires. Do not offer the parts of your body to sin, as instruments of wickedness, but rather offer yourselves to God, as those who have been brought from death to life; and offer the parts of your body to him as instruments of righteousness' (Rom 6:12–13).

Sin robs your life of spiritual power. So does trying to please God in your own strength. In your humanity it is impossible to please God. To use natural resources is to believe that through effort and hard work you can be effective for God. Paul acknowledges the futility of this when he says: 'I know that nothing good lives in me, that is, in my sinful nature' (Rom 7:18). Jesus had already told his disciples: 'apart from me you can do nothing' (Jn 15:5). Therefore, your own strivings need to go to the cross so that you can reach out to receive God's divine strength. It is the exchanged life that is the powerful life. 'I have been crucified with Christ and I no longer live, but Christ lives in me' (Gal 2:20).

The cross is the place of discipleship

Why all this talk about the cross? Discipleship takes the work of the cross yet another step. Jesus said: 'If anyone would come after me, he must deny himself and take up his cross daily and follow me. For whoever wants to save his life will lose it, but whoever loses his life for me will save it.' (Lk 9:23–24).

A leader is first and foremost a disciple. The fact is that all leadership is middle-leadership, because you are only exercising authority on behalf of Another. As a disciple of Jesus Christ, your life will encourage others to become disciples too.

Where then does the cross come in? The phrase 'take up your cross' is often misused in everyday language to refer to some burden or misfortune that we have to carry around with us like the dead albatross around the neck of the Ancient Mariner. This entirely misrepresents the meaning of the Scripture. To 'take up your cross daily' is to be so completely a disciple of Jesus that everything in your life that is contrary to the will of God 'goes to the cross daily' so that the life of Jesus is seen in you.

In these verses Jesus spells out the terms of following him. It begins with 'denying self'. In your human nature you want to please yourself, and do what *you* want to do. As a Christian, you want to do things *for* God; but that is not discipleship. To 'deny self' is to turn away from self-pleasing and all the self-sins that so easily dominate—self-will, self-righteousness, self-esteem, self-consciousness, selfishness, to name but a few—and to follow after Jesus and do his will. But between the denying of self and the following of Jesus stands the cross. It is through the power of the death of Jesus that it is possible for you to be a true disciple of Jesus. Of your human nature you do not want to forsake all the self-sins in

74

your life. But Jesus said: 'whoever wants to save his life will lose it'.

Discipleship is a place of freedom and joy, not of deprivation. Jesus also said: 'whoever loses his life for me will save it'. To live the life God intends you to live is completely fulfilling, but it is costly and will demand all that you are and have. Paul testifies to the way in which the call to discipleship gripped his life:

> But whatever was to my profit I now consider loss for the sake of Christ. What is more, I consider everything a loss compared to the surpassing greatness of knowing Christ Jesus my Lord, for whose sake I have lost all things. I consider them rubbish, that I may gain Christ (Phil 3:7–8).

The cross of Jesus releases you from bondage to a life of self-pleasing and sets you free to become a slave of Christ— 'whose service is perfect freedom'.

The cross principle

To discover the breadth and inexhaustible riches in the work of the cross is to want to live there. As those called to ministry and leadership, our lives must continually point to the cross and be indelibly stamped with the cross, because: 'from him and through him and to him are all things' (Rom 11:36).

The cross is where our pilgrimage both begins and ends. As Paul writes:

> But we have this treasure in jars of clay to show that this all-surpassing power is from God and not from us. We are hard pressed on every side, but not crushed; perplexed, but not in despair; persecuted, but not abandoned; struck down, but not destroyed. We always carry around in our body the death of Jesus, so that the life of Jesus may also be revealed in our body. For we who are alive are always being given over to death for Jesus' sake, so that his life may be revealed in our mortal body. So then, death is at work in us, but life is at work in you (2 Cor 4:7–12).

Here the work of the cross is portrayed as a refining fire in the life of a Christian. As one called to ministry, I am always wanting God to do more through me. How will my ministry become more powerful? This scripture shows that the more the death of Jesus is seen in my life, the more the life of Jesus will be at work in those whom I serve. The whole of my life is the crucible in which God deals with me. His fire tests me through pressure, perplexity, persecution, and by being struck down.

Is God trying to put me through some form of punishment? Not at all. What I find is that these things are not unusual happenings or something unique for Christians, but they are simply the circumstances of life. Satan would want to make capital out of them and destroy me with them, but as I apply the work of Calvary to my life God employs them to mature, refine and enable me to become more usable in his hands. Is the cross doing a refining work in your life?

The first time I visited The Hyde it was June. In the drawing-room and the library there are large open grates where log fires burn during the winter months. I was surprised to find in each grate a bed of ashes about four inches deep which had not been cleared out. My initial reaction was to get a bucket and shovel and remove them. However, I restricted myself to asking why the ashes remained. The answer was that when burning logs in such a large grate it is essential to have a deep bed of ashes. As the logs burn, the ashes heat up and increase the warmth that is thrown out into the room.

Later, at a Leaders' Week, the drawing-room fire became an allegory. The Lord showed me that the grate with the log fire is a picture of our lives. As each circumstance and trial is encountered and brought to the cross, it is dealt with and becomes like ashes in the bed of our lives. Rather than these situations working against us, when they are taken to the cross and burnt up in its fire, their ashes act as a reflector for the glory of God to shine through us to others.

In a book about Joseph, Dr J. R. Miller said: 'Whole, unbruised, unbroken men are of little use to God' (quoted in

Paul E. Billheimer, *The Mystery of His Providence*, Kingsway Publications 1983). Do not despise the testings or the ashes that result. The principle of the cross is: 'Death is at work in us, but life is at work in you' (2 Cor 4:12).

A poem that God gave to Paula Worth, a member of the Fellowship, speaks graphically of the continuing work of the cross in our lives:

The Reason for the Fire

Within this frail vessel lies
The crucible wherein my faith is tested.
The refiner alone knows how delicate is his task;
The flame must be neither so low that dross remains,
Nor yet so high that the fragile beauty of the crucible
Is shattered for ever in its heat.
And so steadily and gently he applies his fire,
His only motive my purification;
His purpose not wavering,
His eyes fixed on the beauty that he will one day behold...
Regarding nonetheless my present suffering with compassion,
The identification of one who has also walked in the fire
And proved that it does not utterly consume,
Even if it should include a Calvary.
As in my fire I cry out to him
And see him walking freely towards me,
I realize afresh that only in the fire
Are my bonds burned away;
And I receive a heart poured through with love,
His love to stand with others in their fire,
Until in that final purity
We stand together at his throne.

7

A Man Who Hears God

'I do not seem to be able to hear God.' At the beginning of almost every Leaders' Week someone will speak out those words or similar. They may be in the form of a question: 'Will you teach me how to hear God?'

How to hear God

One major area of Satan's attack is to make you believe that you cannot hear God. Why? Because he is afraid of those who live in vital contact with God. It is only when you live in constant communication with the living God that your life and ministry can advance with purpose and confidence.

Similarly, that is the reason why in both war and peace, radio and telecommunications are so vital. When a *coup* takes place in some Third World nation, the first thing that is captured is the radio station. If you have possession of the communications network you are in control.

The truth is that every Christian can hear God. You cannot become a Christian without having heard God. Jesus said: 'I tell you the truth, whoever hears my word and believes him who sent me has eternal life and will not be condemned; he has crossed over from death to life' (Jn 5:24). Every child of God can go back in his mind to the time when God spoke—through a sermon or a book or through the testimony of another—and he responded to his call and was born again.

When you are born into the new life of Jesus, it is as though a radio receiver has been planted within you by the Holy Spirit. You now belong to him, and he wants to speak to you

78

and hear from you. His voice is not an isolated thing, for he desires real friendship and fellowship with you.

How can you have the assurance that God will speak to you and that you will hear him? First, because he has told you through his word: 'He who belongs to God hears what God says' (Jn 8:47).

Secondly, on examination of the experience of your own life you will discover that you have already heard God many times and in many ways. However, if at this present time you are not hearing God, it may be that discouragement or disobedience have blocked your spiritual ears.

Thirdly, you will discover as this chapter unfolds that you may have neglected and perhaps rejected the many ways God has already been using to try to get through to you.

When listening to God it is important to realize that he speaks most often with that 'still small voice' and you need to take time to learn to become sensitive to that voice. I can pick out the voice of my wife or one of the children in a crowded room because I have learned to recognize their particular pitch and tone. If you play a musical instrument, say a flute, you can hear the notes of the flute even while listening to a full orchestra with all the instruments playing. Your ear is tuned to pick out the flute. Listening to God is like that. We must learn to pick out the sound of his voice in the midst of a noisy world.

Every child of God can hear the voice of God. But for those called by God to leadership in his church it is even more important to hear him every day; in fact, it is *vital* that you live in constant contact with him.

Hearing God through his word

The Bible is central to all our listening to God. God speaks to us through his word and we need to live in it daily if we are to remain in the centre of his will. All that we hear in other ways needs to be tested by the Scriptures. All the words that we receive from God need to be in harmony with his holy word. The Bible is the revelation of the triune God to his own people. It is not merely a doctrinal statement concerning the

Christian life or a history of God's people.

The Pharisees had the same Scriptures as Jesus did; yet they made it a code that bound both themselves and their followers so that Jesus said to them: 'You diligently study the Scriptures because you think that by them you possess eternal life. These are the Scriptures that testify about me, yet you refuse to come to me to have life' (Jn 5:39–40).

Contrast that with the scene on the Emmaus road when we see Jesus handling the same Scriptures. 'And beginning with Moses and all the Prophets, he explained to them what was said in all the Scriptures concerning himself' (Lk 24:27). And notice the response of those two disciples when they realized the identity of their travelling companion: 'Were not our hearts burning within us while he talked with us on the road and opened the Scriptures to us? (v.32.)

You will see that it is possible to read the Bible without necessarily hearing God. How then do we hear him through the Scriptures? It begins with faith and expectancy. Faith believes that God wants to speak each day through the Scriptures. Expectancy believes that he will speak *today*, because God is always true to his word.

I believe we need to read the Scriptures in a number of different ways. First, we need to soak in the word. 'As the rain and the snow come down from heaven, and do not return to it without watering the earth and making it bud and flourish, so that it yields seed for the sower and bread for the eater, so is my word' (Is 55:10–11).

It is good to read large chunks of the Bible. I find it useful to be working through a book of the Old Testament, a psalm, one of the Gospels and an epistle, reading through a chapter or more at a time and allowing the word to wash over me like rain. I may not find any particular verse that jumps out of the page, but I find that I am refreshed and cleansed by the experience.

Secondly, we need to meditate on the word. Personally, I do this in two ways. When reading through the Scriptures I have a system of marking with coloured pencils, each colour referring to a particular theme or topic. This is not just to produce a multi-coloured Bible, but is an aid to concentration and also provides a useful key for following through various themes and principles in the Scriptures. Another kind of meditation I use is to take just one verse or phrase and allow it to sink into my mind and spirit and ask God to bring it alive within me.

There are many other ways of reading the Bible, but these three methods are particularly appropriate to hearing God through his word. It is important to be reading the Bible as a regular daily discipline and not only as preparation for sermons and the like. When reading in the ways outlined above I find that avenues are opened up through which God can speak to me. The psalmist says: 'Your word is a lamp to my feet and a light for my path' (Ps 119:105).

Hearing God as we wait in his presence

'I want all the Fellowship to make it a daily practice to set aside time to listen to God and to write down in a notebook what he is saying.' Colin Urquhart was speaking to the whole Fellowship and had been teaching on the principles of listening to God. He had made this particular practice a part of his own life for many years.

I remember that my first reaction was very negative. For a start, writing down things that God spoke today seemed to suggest that the Bible was incomplete. And what was more, I could not really believe that I could hear God.

As I talked these things over with Colin I learned that what was written down was similar to prophecy, which the Scriptures teach is not an addition to the Bible but given, as Paul writes 'for strengthening, encouragement and comfort' (1 Cor 14:3). Like prophecy, anything heard and written down is not perfect but needs to be tested by the body of Christ: 'For we know in part and we prophesy in part' (1 Cor 13:9).

I also had to realize that when Jesus said 'He who belongs to God hears what God says,' this included me and that I too could hear God.

And so I began. At the beginning of my daily time of quiet with God, I simply prayed: 'Father, will you speak to me concerning my life today and about your will for me?' I picked up my pen and began to write. I did not hear an audible voice, but just had a sense that certain things were being impressed upon me. I wrote them down. I wrote about six lines in my book. Looking over what I had written, I felt a little foolish. Had I made it up? Had God really spoken to me? I closed the book and began to read the Scriptures and to pray concerning the day ahead, thinking no more about what I had written.

The next morning I felt a little discouraged at the thought of continuing this exercise and somewhat reluctantly opened up the notebook. As I read over the previous day's writing I was amazed. What I had written down was totally appropriate to what had happened the day before. God *had* spoken! A sense of joy and relief flowed over me and I eagerly reached out for my pen and quietly waited for God to speak again.

Listening to God daily has now become a most productive and creative part of my life. I believe it is vital for all who are called to leadership and ministry to cultivate this regular habit of waiting quietly in God's presence and listening to his voice. 'Blessed is the man who listens to me, watching daily at my doors, waiting at my doorway' (Prov 8:34).

Let me give some advice and sound some warnings about this exercise. The words received are personal and no one, not even my wife, reads what I have written. I do not quote my notebook to others to direct their lives. The things given are spoken into my own life. If I do share what I have heard it will be in order to receive confirmation or otherwise from the body.

As I sit quietly before God, the first thing he shows me is any unconfessed sin. This leads me to repentance. When I am out of sorts with God or my family I find it very difficult to come before him, as I know I will hear nothing until I have put things right both with him and others.

Waiting quietly in the presence of God is not a passive exercise. If I am having a conversation with a person there is always a two-way flow. If I want answers from God, I need to ask him questions. So I present the various situations in my life to God and ask what I need to know about them. On some issues I hear an immediate answer which I write down. Other questions may well remain unanswered, which does not concern me greatly because I do not have a right to demand an answer from God. I know that his answer will come when the time is right. What I do is to keep asking the same question and I discover as the days go by that God does unfold his answer and his direction as I continue in faithful obedience to him. If I am not getting through I may well be asking the wrong questions.

I seldom read back more than one or two days and dispense with my notebook when it is full. To look back places more emphasis on past words than on the freshness of God's voice for today. If I find it difficult to hear anything, I do glance back a day or two to discover things God has said that I have failed to obey. I find God will not waste words on the disobedient. I know that what I write is not perfect, so I do not put too much weight on one day's writing, but find that the things God repeatedly says to me are most important. In the Fellowship to which I belong, hearing and writing down is a common practice so there is no question of spiritual pride arising on account of hearing God—because we all hear him.

What I am hearing will be in harmony with what God is saying to my fellow leaders. At times it will be new and demanding, but if it is of God it will be recognized as such by all of us as it is shared.

Time spent quietly in the presence of God is essential for developing a listening ear and certainly writing in a notebook is not the only way of hearing him. Whenever pressures escalate it is good to get away into a quiet place and allow God to minister peace into our hearts and to speak into the situation. Time given to him is never wasted. 'He wakens me morning by morning, wakens my ear to listen like one being taught' (Is 50:4).

Hearing God in the circumstances of life

You will be saying: 'You have just told us to withdraw from the circumstances of life to hear God. Now you are telling us to hear God in the circumstances.' That is right.

As leadership reproduces itself, your own situation will give you an indication of what your leadership is producing.

During a Leaders' Week some time ago I happened to say: 'If you want to see what you are like as a leader, take a look at your people—they are a reflection of you.' The effect was dramatic! One man let out an involuntary cry that said it all. Through it he heard God and realized that as God dealt with him, he would in turn deal with the people. That is exactly what has happened. As God has poured more of his life and Spirit into that man, his church has come to experience new life and power.

Listening to God is not a head-in-the-clouds affair. It must always be firmly rooted in reality. Becoming aware of the circumstances is not to be overwhelmed by them, but to see where faith needs to work. There are times when we look at what has happened and cry out: 'It has all gone wrong, nothing good can come out of this.' This is where the foundation of the word is vital to produce the endurance of faith and an absolute assurance of the sovereignty of God.

Paul says: 'And we know that in all things God works for the good of those who love him, who have been called according to his purpose' (Rom 8:28). God has allowed it to happen, it has not taken him by surprise, and his promise is that he is working for the good of those who love him. That is where faith is built, upon the foundation of the Bible. Having acknowledged that fact, we can reach out to God to receive from him the answer to the situation. He is always the God who redeems. As the psalmist declares: 'with the Lord is unfailing love and with him is full redemption' (Ps 130:7).

Amy Carmichael has said: 'Nothing anyone can do to us can injure us unless we submit to a wrong reaction.' I found the quotation in a book about the life of Joseph who had thirteen very difficult years in which to hear God in the circumstances. When he recalls those years at the end of his life, he speaks to his brothers who were responsible for selling him into slavery and says: 'You intended to harm me, but God intended it for good to accomplish what is now being done, the saving of many lives' (Gen 50:20).

There are times when circumstances tell us we are in the

wrong place or doing the wrong thing. God's word assures us that as we obediently and faithfully follow him we will know peace, fruitfulness and direction. The psalmist says: 'Great peace have they who love your law, and nothing can make them stumble' (Ps 119:165). Peace is not the absence of conflict, but a gift of God in the midst of the hurly burly of life. If having faithfully followed through the principles of listening to God and seeking him daily we are left with a great lack of peace, we may well ask: 'What is God trying to say to me?' It is important to check out this restlessness with the person under whose authority you operate, because it can occur for a number of different reasons. A lack of peace is one way in which we hear God. It may be over some small thing that needs to be put right, but it may be on account of something important that has a bearing on the whole direction of our lives.

Jesus said: 'You did not choose me, but I chose you to go and bear fruit—fruit that will last' (Jn 15:16). Fruitlessness may well indicate that something is wrong. Sometimes faithfulness is confused with fruitfulness. God does call his people to live faithfully before him, but he also wants their lives to be fruitful. According to your calling you should be seeing fruit to the glory of God. If there is little or none to be seen you need to do some serious talking with God.

Of all men, leaders need to know where they are going. If they have no purpose or direction, neither will those who are led. To be the blind leading the blind has always been a disastrous occupation. If you know your life to be aimless, you need to come before God fearlessly to hear what he has to say and be prepared to obey him.

Hearing God through the gifts of the Holy Spirit

'Now to each one the manifestation of the Spirit is given for the common good' (1 Cor 12:7). God has placed his Holy Spirit within us to give us his power, love, holiness and joy. The Holy Spirit within is also like the radio receiver I wrote about earlier. He enables us to receive knowledge and understanding that cannot be gained by natural means.

The gifts of the Holy Spirit may be given during times of personal prayer, the most likely being prophecy, visions or words of knowledge. But they are more often experienced when the body of believers meets together for worship and prayer. Whether they are received individually or corporately they are always for the common good, that is, for the building up of the body of Christ.

Prophecy is a word from God that brings strengthening, encouragement or comfort. God may also speak in this way through the gift of tongues which will be followed by the interpretation. It does not necessarily predict future events, but brings God's people direction, guidance and, very often, a challenge.

A prophetic word may come in the form of a picture or vision. I believe God uses this pictorial form when it is especially important that the message needs to be remembered, as it is far easier to remember a picture than words. The person to whom it is given will see in their imagination either a static picture or an unfolding scene which they then describe in words.

We have often found that as the team is praying about a forthcoming Leaders' Week, God will give a prophecy or vision to someone which helps us to focus in prayer on needs that cannot be known in any other way.

A word of knowledge is a truth that God knows about a person and that is unknown to the one who is praying. God pulls back the curtain on his knowledge so that he can reveal hidden factors that are important to the situation in hand. A classic example of this can be seen in John's Gospel, when Jesus is having a conversation with the woman of Samaria. Jesus said to her: '"Go, call your husband and come back." "I have no husband," she replied. Jesus said to her, "You are right when you say you have no husband. The fact is, you have had five husbands, and the man you now have is not your husband"' (Jn 4:16–18). Jesus spoke out of knowledge that had been received from God. It broke the situation open and resulted in the woman's life being transformed, and those of many others who heard her testimony (v.39).

During a Leaders' Week we were having a time of prayer

and waiting upon God when I received a word of knowledge which I spoke out. 'There is someone here, I believe, who has a fear which has a real grip on you and is connected with your mother. God wants to set you free.' Immediately a woman spoke out: 'My grandmother became senile before she reached sixty and so did my mother. I have been told since childhood that women in our family become senile before they reach sixty. I am over 50 and am gripped by a fear of senility.' I asked her to come to the front of the meeting and in Jesus' name I rebuked the fear and she was immediately released. But, more importantly, when I saw her some months later at our Family Camp she looked ten years younger and was still rejoicing in the freedom she had received.

Praise God for the gifts he gives that bring understanding and help in hearing his voice.

Hearing God by listening to people

There is a great deal of difference between living in fear of people's reactions and listening to them in a creative way. Paul said: 'Am I now trying to win the approval of men, or of God? Or am I trying to please men? If I were still trying to please men, I would not be a servant of Christ' (Gal 1:10).

In listening to the people under my leadership, the first question I ask is: 'What are you hearing from God?' Listening to God is not something that can happen in isolation, because revelation received from God needs to be tested by the body of Christ. The fact is that if what I have been hearing is really from God, then others around me will probably be hearing the same thing. This provides encouragement and confirmation.

What happens, though, if the body is hearing something that is in contrast to that heard by the leadership? Personally, I trust that I am always approachable and able to receive correction and rebuke, for the leader should be the most submitted person of all. If, however, my people found me unreceptive to their approaches they could always speak to my fellow elders who would test what was being said and together we would seek the mind of God. This could well correct us and cause us to seek the forgiveness of the body.

The danger of leadership being centred in one person is that when he is unable to receive valid insights from the body it can only result in weakness and dislocation. That is one reason why I believe that leadership should always be corporate.

It is in its unity and openness to hearing God through even the weakest vessel that the body will advance with purpose and strength.

Paul writing to the Corinthians says: 'For no matter how many promises God has made, they are "Yes" in Christ. And so through him the "Amen" is spoken by us to the glory of God' (2 Cor 1:20).

As we hear what God is saying and as we declare it to the people, we can expect to hear the 'Amen' as each one receives it as from God.

As well as listening to what others are hearing from God, it is important to listen out in a general way to comments and reactions. I find my children are worth listening to when I want to hear God. Children respond spontaneously and without mincing their words, and are fine judges of character and spirituality. If someone is staying in my home who has no genuine spirituality but is merely pretending, the children have them rumbled in no time.

We need to cultivate a godly awareness of the people and situations that surround us. I find that the exercise of working in a team listening to God with others has a sharpening effect on me. I can share what I am hearing from God and hear from them what they have been receiving. This practice shows up the things that are from my own imagination and not from God.

In my early days with the Bethany Fellowship, the eldership consisted of Colin Urquhart, David Brown and myself. We used to set aside days to pray together and work through the situation facing us. Often Colin would say: 'Let's not talk about these various issues. We will each go away to pray about them and listen to what God is saying, then come together again to say what we have heard.' I found this tremendously challenging and very rewarding. I learned so much about listening quietly to God. As we came back to share what we had heard the unity was remarkable, but even more remarkable was the fact that on many occasions we came to a conclusion completely opposite to that which would have emerged from discussion. You can only learn by doing.

Hearing God by the peace he gives

'For God is not a God of disorder but of peace' (1 Cor 14:33). These words were spoken by Paul to the Corinthians and refer particularly to orderliness in worship. The truth of that sentence also reaches into the realm of listening to God. When we have heard God about any situation of life or ministry, 'peace' is a great test as to whether what we have been hearing is really God's answer.

Paul says: 'Let the peace of Christ rule in your hearts, since as members of one body you were called to peace' (Col 3:15). At an individual level I can ask myself: 'Have I got the Lord's peace about this?' My response is a good check on whether it is from God or not.

Jesus said: 'Peace I leave with you; my peace I give you. I do not give to you as the world gives. Do not let your hearts be troubled and do not be afraid' (Jn 14:27). Peace is one of the characteristics of the Spirit and should be a hallmark of godly leadership.

That same peace can also be found in corporate decision-making. If all the principles of listening to God are followed, decisions need never be made by voting because all those whose responsibility it is to make them will be hearing God and will have arrived at the same conclusion. I do not say that lightly. I know there are committees where the variable level of spiritual sensitivity would rule out unanimous decisions. However, I do not believe that those who are responsible for the spiritual leadership of the people of God, for example elders, should ever reach their decisions by voting. The exercise of reaching the decision may well involve much prayer and exchange of views, but it will end in a place of peace where God's voice has been clearly heard and where all are in complete accord. This is the way we operate in the Bethany Fellowship.

When corporate spiritual leadership does not reach decisions through prayer and waiting upon God in addition to frank discussion, there will be inherent weakness. Majority decisions leave the minority unconvinced. Making united decisions will always require sacrifice from every member of the leadership. Entrenched positions are a mark of bigotry not spiritual maturity.

Some time ago I was invited to a church that was torn by division. Over a period of about eighteen months polarization had taken place among both the people and the leadership. Majority decisions had been totally ineffective and there had been a steady stream of people leaving and joining other churches. I was asked to speak to a group of leaders and members and after listening to all points of view I could see no common ground. Yet I knew that this strife was not what God desired for his people. I recommended that they came together simply to seek God and meet with him in his holiness. It is in repentance at the foot of the cross where unity is born. 'If you are ready to meet with God, he will redeem your situation and give you a new future. God will bring you all to repentance, and lead you to a completely new attitude to his purpose and to one another,' I said in closing. Later one of the elders phoned me to report a meeting that had produced little repentance and no unity. That church cannot survive if the situation remains.

It is only when the greatness of God's majesty overcomes the smallness of man's opinions that we have the key to unity. This is the principle of revival (see Chapter 5).

God's revelation for life and ministry

'Where there is no vision the people perish' (Prov 29:18 av). There is much more to hearing God than just receiving guidance for your own daily walk with him. You need to receive from him such a revelation of his word and purpose that you lead the people with a real sense of assurance and confidence in God.

There is a very interesting translation of that verse in Proverbs in the New International Version. It says: 'Where there is no revelation, the people cast off restraint.' The people of God need to know that their leaders are hearing from God about his plans for them as individuals, and for them as a church. Where this is absent the people become restless and tend to make independent decisions. I trust that the teaching in Chapter 4 will have been sufficient warning about the perils of independence!

There is a tremendous amount of unrest and dissatisfaction today, even in many seemingly alive churches. Why? Because there is no revelation. The people are not confident that their leaders are really hearing from God.

God's people need leadership because God has a purpose for them. Those in leadership will find God if they seek him and discover that purpose—God's revelation to his people.

I recommend that you read carefully Jeremiah 23:16–29. The prophet is showing the difference between the words of lying prophets and the word of God. The lying prophets bring false hopes and visions from their own minds, but God brings revelation through his dynamic, powerful word. '"Is not my word like fire," declares the Lord, "and like a hammer that breaks a rock in pieces?"' (Jer 23:29).

8

A Man Who Lives His Message

We in our Western society have been greatly influenced by Greek philosophy which seeks to divide our lives into compartments. In Greek thought the spiritual is separated from the physical; the sacred from the secular. Put into practice in our society this has had some alarming and damaging consequences. The effect on those in leadership has been to separate the function of ministry from the rest of life. This can mean that we concentrate upon one aspect of our work, say for example preaching, and believe that the better prepared we are and the more thought and effort we put into our sermons, the more effective they will be. The truth is that if our lives are in contradiction to our words, the sermon is of minimal worth and will not touch people's hearts however much work has been expended on it.

It may also be that we have a much sought-after counselling ministry and give all the hours we can to praying with and helping others. If this means that our partners and families are neglected and suffer, the dynamic of that ministry will be short lived.

The writer to the Hebrews says: 'Consider the outcome of their way of life' (Heb 13:7). Here again is the basic principle at the heart of this book—leadership is by example. Jesus is our supreme example. He came to be not only the atoning sacrifice for our sins and to reconcile men to God, but also to demonstrate a holy life. Jesus was speaking about behaviour towards friends, family and enemies when he said: 'Be perfect, therefore, as your heavenly Father is perfect' (Mt 5:48).

Holiness is positive, not negative

There is a misunderstanding of holiness that places people under a heavy weight of negatives. By the time Jesus appeared on the scene many hundreds of petty restrictions had been added by the Pharisees to the original laws given by God to Moses. It was virtually impossible to obey all the additional laws; and they caused much hardship and totally misrepresented God's character.

If we are labouring under the misconception that our lives are divided, our 'holiness' will be a false piety issuing in religious practices that have no relevance to life, and the other compartments of our life will also be dishonouring to God. It is God's purpose that our lives have a harmony that brings glory to him and bears fruit in the lives of others.

In order to be more holy, I may retreat to a hut on a mountainside and spend many days in prayer and meditation. When I return to my church and family the test of my holiness will not be my pious words or holy countenance but my reaction when someone treads on my toe!

The acid test of true revival and holiness is its effect on every area of my being. Jesus was not only known for his preaching and miracles, but for his holiness. As a child it was said of him: 'And Jesus grew in wisdom and stature, and in favour with God and men' (Lk 2:52). Peter testifies to the perfection of Jesus' life when he recalls the words of Isaiah: 'He committed no sin, and no deceit was found in his mouth' (1 Pet 2:22). He then goes on to add his own comment: 'When they hurled their insults at him, he did not retaliate; when he suffered, he made no threats' (v.23).

To be holy is to be like Jesus. To be like Jesus is to live his message. How can this be? It is possible to be so filled with the holy presence of Jesus as we seek him daily, live in his word and commune with him in prayer that his life is lived in us.

Holiness is positive and when God fills us with his Holy Spirit it is so that we can live the life he intended for us. In recent years there has been great emphasis on the work of the Holy Spirit releasing power, faith, gifts and healing. This has tended to mask the truth that God also gives us his Spirit for holiness and to produce the fruit of the Spirit with its ninefold characteristics of love, joy, peace, patience, kindness, goodness, faithfulness, gentleness and self-control.

Living the message in my own life

As a leader, your life is under scrutiny as well as your work for God. The Scriptures give some very clear teaching about this. If you are called to be a minister, elder or deacon, or to hold some other responsibility of spiritual leadership, you need to consider carefully the standards that have been set for you. If you are choosing someone to fulfil a particular office or function you need to recognize the principles laid down and to remember that you have no right to choose anyone on any other grounds or criteria.

Overseers in the letter to Timothy seem to be the same as elders in Titus: those who have the pastoral leadership of the church; people of maturity and integrity who teach and exercise authority. The character of deacons is outlined in Paul's first letter to Timothy and their function is more clearly defined in Acts 6:1–6. They seem to be chosen not only for their godliness but for their ability to perform the practical functions of the church.

This is the scriptural list of qualities required:

An overseer must be:—
    above reproach
    the husband of one wife
    temperate
    self-controlled
    respectable
    hospitable
    able to teach
    not given to much wine
    not violent but gentle
    not quarrelsome
    not a lover of money
    managing his own family well

obeyed with proper respect by his children
not a recent convert
enjoying a good reputation with outsiders

(1 Tim 3:1–7)

A deacon must be:—
worthy of respect
sincere
not indulging in much wine
not pursuing dishonest gain
keeping hold of the deep truths of the faith
tested before being appointed
the husband of one wife
managing his children and household well

(1 Tim 3:8–13)

An elder must be:—
blameless
the husband of one wife
a man whose children believe
a man whose children are not wild and disobedient
not overbearing
not quick-tempered
not given to much wine
not violent
not pursuing dishonest gain
hospitable
one who loves what is good
self-controlled
upright
holy and disciplined
holding firmly to the trustworthy message
encouraging others by sound doctrine
refuting those who oppose the teaching

(Tit 1:6–9)

Your message is your lifestyle. This needs the mark of God upon it, so that whatever you do or say, your life is bringing glory to God.

Paul is bold enough to say of himself: 'Therefore I urge you to imitate me. For this reason I am sending to you Timothy, my son whom I love, who is faithful in the Lord. He will remind you of my way of life in Christ Jesus, which agrees with what I teach everywhere in every church' (1 Cor 4: 16–17).

While constantly urging people to be like Jesus, Paul realizes that as a leader he needs to set an example by being like Jesus himself, so that he can say: 'Follow my example, as I follow the example of Christ' (1 Cor 11:1).

This is an important, practical and yet often neglected teaching. It will not be learned by subjecting yourself to rigorous rules and regulations. Although it does require spiritual discipline and obedience, it calls even more for a step of faith in allowing God to pour his refining Spirit over every area of your life.

Living the message in my marriage

'Husbands love your wives' (Eph 5:25). Fidelity in marriage is a principle for those called to lead others. My own marriage is the primary place of openness in my life. It is the first place where I need to walk in the light in the way John teaches in his first letter. To confess my faults to the one who knows me humanly best of all liberates me to be open in repentance before my children, my household and the rest of the body of Christ.

Joyce is the one with whom I share the strongest bond of unity, stronger even than with my fellow elders. That makes our relationship a powerful place of prayer. Jesus said: 'I tell you that if two of you on earth agree about anything you ask for, it will be done for you by my father in heaven' (Mt 18:19). Agreeing in prayer is not merely a formula of words but is a powerful dynamic that flows out of hearts that are in vital unity.

In Peter's first letter he is exhorting men to be considerate as they live with their wives, not only because a man should be loving and caring, but also because a lack of consideration will hinder prayer (1 Pet 3:7).

I thank God for a warm, loving and mutually satisfying physical relationship in my marriage, based on giving and not on getting. This brings joy and strength to us both and denies the enemy a channel of temptation. It is tragic that many people called to Christian leadership have made shipwreck of their lives through moral sin. Often the reason is not simply insufficient resistance to the temptation, but lack of time given to building a strong and satisfying sexual relationship within the marriage. As someone has said: 'If there is peace in the bedroom there will be peace in the home.'

The other day I was listening to a cassette and was struck by these words: 'The first need of a Christian wife is to have a man whose heart is after God.' What was being said was that you need to love God more than you love your wife. If you love God more than you love your wife, you will love your wife better than if the order were reversed. Your love is imperfect and often self-centred, whereas God's love is pure, holy and selfless. As you love him more, his love will be poured through you to your wife and beyond to your family and all the others he has given you to love.

I believe it to be very important for a wife to know the call of God on her life in the same way that her husband does. That call will not be at variance with his so that it creates conflict, but will have come to her direct from God.

Let me illustrate. In June 1979 God made it clear that he was directing me to leave Cornwall and move to Sussex to become part of the Bethany Fellowship. It was very important for me to know that Joyce had received the same call. We were in complete unity, knowing that God had spoken to us both, and were therefore eager and ready to go. We were then able to share this with our children for whom the move was also costly as schools had to be changed and friends left behind. The unity God gave Joyce and me paved the way for family unity, and we all came willingly together.

I have seen men lose a God-given ministry when their wives have undermined their vision, obedience and determination. It is not practical in Christian ministry and leadership for a couple to work on the 'you go your way and I'll go mine' principle. The result of that kind of situation will inevitably be weakness and failure. Let it also be said that I have seen women whose commitment to God's call on their lives has been stunted by their husbands!

Living the message in my family

'Fathers, do not exasperate your children: instead, bring them up in the training and instruction of the Lord' (Eph 6:4). It is all too easy to neglect the family when there are many other pressures. Yet my home is the place where I live the message most frequently and the fruit of it should be evident there. This will not happen by chance.

God has given me the responsibility of training my children in the ways of God. The word of God promises: 'Train a child in the way he should go, and when he is old he will not turn from it' (Prov 22:6).

I have five children whose ages range at the time of writing from 8 to 18. I praise God that they are normal, healthy children. They all have a personal faith in Jesus and have been filled with the Holy Spirit. That does not mean they are perfect or that they always find Sunday worship exciting! But it does mean that they have a simple and honest faith in God.

As their father, I need to see that Joyce has time to care for them and is not constantly pulled away on other ministry demands. It is my responsibility to see that we pray together and read the Bible regularly as a family. It is also important to be ready to answer the doubts and questions that arise as they grow and develop as people.

Because of the demands of God's call on my life, my children know that it means sacrifice for them as well as for Joyce, in that they will not see as much of me as they would like. It is up to me to set the standards of behaviour and obedience in our home so that Joyce can exercise authority on my behalf when I am not there. I need to guard the free time I do get in making sure that I have a real relationship with each of them. I am only too aware of my own limitations, but I truly desire to fulfil my responsibilities as their father faithfully and lovingly.

In our home there are other members of the family in addition to the children. In the Bethany Fellowship we live in extended households and single people become members of a household and therefore members of the family. Rosie, David and Lyn are part of my family as well as Joyce's father who is over 80.

An extended family is a wonderful place of warmth, love, healing and enrichment. It is also demanding for all concerned as we learn to love and care for one another, and it is all too easy for those beyond one's natural family to feel like lodgers. I know that God had to teach me deep lessons about this. In our first year in the Fellowship we had two others join our household and as far as I could see we were all very happy. However, after many months I realized that my relationship with them was cool and shallow—in fact, I had failed to establish a really meaningful rapport with either of them.

I was pondering this when I came across a verse in Philippians that seemed to give me the key. Paul is speaking warmly about the Christians in Philippi and his prayers and aspirations for them. He then says this: 'It is right for me to feel this way about all of you, since I have you in my heart' (Phil 1:7). I know now that I failed to make a place in my heart for those other members of my household.

I asked God to forgive me for my remoteness and to give me a real love for all those who were part of my family. I am glad to say that God changed my heart. Rosie was one of those who spent that first year in our home. She then moved to another household, only to return to us two and a half years later. Rosie was with me during one of the Ministry Weeks at The Hyde and heard me testify to what God had revealed. On the way home she said, 'I can really confirm the truth of what you were saying this morning because you were so different when I returned to your household.' David is also a member both of my team during Leaders' Weeks and my household, and is able to verify the consistency of my message. I know that he has the right to contradict anything that I preach if I am not seeking to live it out at home. It has a very purifying effect upon me.

Praise God he hasn't finished with me yet! I am aware of a constant need to seek God for his love for all those who are part of my family and all those with whom I work closely.

Living the message in my home

As I travel around the country I often stay in the homes of leaders and ministers. I am immediately aware as I enter someone's house whether there is warmth, love and a welcome. One of the principles of leadership is to be 'hospitable'.

I must see that my home and family learn how to practise hospitality. I like the opening verses of Mark 2: 'when Jesus again entered Capernaum, the people heard that he had come home. So many gathered that there was no room left' (Mk 2:1–2). It is not only when we have guests to stay that our home needs to be a welcoming place, but the whole atmosphere needs to hold out an invitation for people to 'drop in'.

As the Holy Spirit flows through the lives of those who live there the love, joy and peace of Jesus will be present. There will also be an order and cleanliness that is honouring to God. Cleanliness is supposed to be close to godliness! However, that does not mean that tidiness and housework should become a fetish—a home needs to be a home and not a set piece for *Ideal Home*.

Our home contains eleven people of all ages which means there will always be a Lego model somewhere to trip over, or a half-made jigsaw puzzle and a partly finished project on the table. But it can still be clean and orderly.

These practical details are important because they often indicate underlying weaknesses. I was invited some time ago to visit a minister who was needing help in sorting out various matters that were causing confusion and disorder among his people. When I entered his study I saw in its untidy state a picture of the spiritual problem that needed dealing with.

The clutter of that study was an indication of the cluttered life of the man which was producing the confusion in his church. James in his letter writes of asking God for the wisdom that will bring clarity and order to life. To doubt and not exercise faith produces double-mindedness which makes a man unstable in all his ways (Jas 1:5–7).

Therefore, as God's revival power flows through your life,

it will change your home, bringing order, love and joy. It will then be a place where your children want to bring their friends, where people want to drop in for a coffee and chat, where guests feel at home and where the holy presence of Jesus dwells.

Living the message in my finances

As God changes your life he will not stop short at your pocket. I have found that the first thing that happens as God moves deeply in the financial areas of life is the desire to tithe. The Scripture is clear: 'Bring the whole tithe into the storehouse' (Mal 3:10). There is something more to tithing than merely obeying Scripture. It is a whole new attitude to money. The fact that God is getting his right portion will affect the way that the rest of your money is spent. Always remember that a tithe is not *any* tenth but the first tenth. Having given that first tenth, God then transforms your attitude to the spending of the remaining nine-tenths. That is often the reason why people testify that after having been faithful in tithing, their money seemed to go further.

Tithing also brings another biblical principle into play: 'Give, and it will be given to you' (Lk 6:38). It is important for a leader to live by these principles of Scripture as well as teaching them to his people.

I have known people who, because they were being paid out of the income of the church that they were leading, failed to tithe into that church. It seemed to them that there was little point in recycling the money: the truth was that a vital spiritual principle was being neglected.

Wherever your finance comes from, God is the ultimate source and he promises to meet all your needs out of his rich resources. He calls upon you to be a generous giver at all times. Paul unfolds this beautifully as he writes to the Corinthians: 'Each man should give what he has decided in his heart to give, not reluctantly or under compulsion, for God loves a cheerful giver. And God is able to make all grace abound to you, so that in all things at all times, having all that you need, you will abound in every good work'

(2 Cor 9:7–8).

God's generous giving into your life will liberate you to be a generous giver, not only financially but in every other area of life. God's righteousness and holiness sharpen your righteousness in practical finance. 'Let no debt remain outstanding, except the continuing debt to love one another' (Rom 13:8). Christians should be renowned for prompt payment of bills. I regret this has not always been true of me, but I do thank him now for the freedom and joy he has given me as I put his principles into practice.

Whether you have a salaried job or no regular income you still need to look to God in faith to supply all your needs. To be able to pray with confidence and trust God means that you need to live in righteousness and to be a giver. If you are failing to follow the principles God gives in Scripture, you cannot expect him to respond to your requests—although he often meets our needs by grace and not according to principle because he is so faithful.

Faith is thanking God before you receive the answer—not afterwards. I remember a little incident not long ago when I was sorting out my finances and realized that I did not have enough to pay the bills that were in my hand. I was just about to have a good moan to the Lord and tell him about my needs and lack of money, when I remembered what had occurred the previous day. I had been going through some photographs of our children, from birth to the present day. As I looked at them I was overwhelmed with thankfulness to God for his goodness in that he had given us five healthy children who had been kept safe and well over the years. I also recalled that in all my life I had never been without food, clothes or a roof over my head.

'Lord, I'm sorry,' I said, 'I have nothing to complain about. I have a lovely wife, healthy children and you have provided for all my needs. Lord, you have been faithful and you are faithful.' I put the bills to one side and went on with other things. Later that day my secretary came to me with a cheque that covered those bills. As usual, having paid the bills, I had nothing in the bank, but I was left with a deep sense of gratitude to God who is always faithful.

God's answers are not always so quick, but I was taught a lesson that day on how to pray with thanksgiving. 'Do not be anxious about anything, but in everything, by prayer and petition, with thanksgiving, present your requests to God' (Phil 4:6).

Living the message in my work

When I was young, and was given some jobs to do by my father which I was not too enthusiastic about, I would be given a clear directive that like it or not it was to be done, and then a word from Ecclesiastes 9:10 to back it up: 'Whatever your hand finds to do, do it with all your might.' Although not feeling very cheerful about it at the time, that verse has done me good. I believe it underlines a principle concerning attitudes to work.

Whether your work is in a business, profession or industry, or whether it is full-time Christian work, I believe that a standard of excellence is required that marks it out from work done by non-Christians. Unfortunately in many situations this is not so. I hear reports of bad time-keeping, of a lack of enthusiasm, of Christians wasting other employees' time by witnessing about their faith. As Christians, our witness is our work, our testimony is our trustworthiness. If a spoken witness is in fact robbing your employer of time, it is working against itself and will in fact do more harm to the gospel than good.

For those of you in full-time Christian ministry there can be shoddiness about your work which dishonours God. Do the services start on time? Is adequate preparation made for each service? Is there a godly diligence about your work? Are you known for going the second mile, or do you have a work-to-rule mentality?

In a recent study that sought to determine which elements were common to most successful leaders, there was only one factor which was seen to be universally true: they all worked hard. They kept longer hours, studied more, and put more effort into self-improvement than those who worked for them (*People, Tasks and Goals—Studies in Christian Leadership*, International Correspondence Institute, 1983).

I believe the acid test of God's deep working in your life is seen beyond the pulpit and prayer meeting and will be measurable in your daily work. Paul knew the conversion of Onesimus the slave of Philemon was more than skin-deep by the way his work-effectiveness had changed. 'Formerly he was useless to you, but now he has become useful both to you and to me' (Philem 11).

Living the message in my leisure

For those called to ministry leisure is important so that the body, mind and spirit are maintained in good condition and the work can be carried out properly. That may sound a bit clinical but it is important because leisure is not an end in itself. Today's society gives a strong emphasis to leisure activities as though they were an end in themselves. Christians need to see leisure in the right perspective and be sure that the way spare time is used is helpful rather than harmful.

We need to have enough physical exercise to keep us fit and healthy so that we are in good condition for the work of God. Each one will choose the kind of exercise to suit himself. It may be a round of golf or a game of squash, but if your golf handicap or the squash tournament becomes more important than the kingdom of God then something is wrong. I normally take a physically vigorous holiday but am not too consistent about exercise the rest of the time. Each of us needs to understand that our bodies are the temple of the Holy Spirit and the temple needs to be cared for.

Jesus said to his disciples at a time when they were tired as a result of their ministry: 'Come with me by yourselves to a quiet place and get some rest' (Mk 6:31). The interesting thing is that when they arrived, they were greeted by 5,000 people! There are times when rest will be denied because of the priority of God's work. Nevertheless, we need to learn how to relax, thus keeping our minds and spirits alive in the Lord.

It is very easy to use the wrong things to help you relax. When you return late at night after a demanding evening of ministry, how do you wind down? The easiest thing to do is to switch on the television and absorb whatever comes at you. This is unpredictable and can be dangerous. Your mind and your spirit need to be refreshed and yet they can so easily be filled with the wrong things. Guard what you see. It is also very easy to indulge in unnecessary food at this time which will fail to meet your real needs.

When you are tired and your spiritual resources are at a low ebb, the flesh demands to be satisfied. If the flesh wins and you indulge in an excess of food or an unhelpful TV programme, your spiritual vitality is in fact damaged and you will enter the following day in a state of weakness which gives the enemy a victory and leaves you needing to win back some lost spiritual territory.

The Scriptures have the answer: 'Whatever is true, whatever is noble, whatever is right, whatever is pure, whatever is lovely, whatever is admirable—if anything is excellent or praiseworthy—think about such things' (Phil 4:8). Therefore, you need to put your methods of relaxation to the test of Scripture.

In the story in Mark's Gospel which tells of the feeding of the 5,000, Jesus goes up into the hills to pray immediately after having dismissed the people. Why? Having given out so much he needed to recharge his spiritual batteries. It is good to have a devotional book on the go for times when you feel like this. I am a great fan of A. W. Tozer, and I like the way he so often writes short chapters. There are times when three pages of Tozer are just what I need to restore my flagging spirit. It is also a great blessing to end the day with a time of prayer with my wife, especially when the demands of ministry have left me feeling worn out.

Another way spiritual health can be affected is by wasting time late at night, failing to get a good night's sleep, and then being unable to get up early next morning to pray. This can throw the whole day into disarray.

I have tried to deal with this area of leisure in some detail because I know it is so easy to indulge in the kind of activities that have the potential for destroying the effectiveness of leadership rather than enabling it.

There is a vital principle underlying the theme of how God wants each one of us to live the message in our lives. Paul tells us in Romans 12 to offer our bodies as living sacrifices, holy and pleasing to God. At the heart of this chapter is the matter of offering my whole life to God in every area so that his holy power can transform all of it. Romans 6:13, 16 says:

> Do not offer the parts of your body to sin, as instruments of wickedness, but rather offer yourselves to God, as those who have been brought from death to life; and offer the parts of your body to him as instruments of righteousness.... Don't you know that when you offer yourselves to someone to obey him as slaves, you are slaves to the one whom you obey—whether you are slaves to sin, which leads to death, or to obedience, which leads to righteousness?

On a glorious, warm sunny day during one of the Leaders' Weeks we met together for a time of worship and prayer, and God led us to do something we had never done before. To begin with I spoke from the two verses in Romans 6 quoted above about offering every compartment of our lives afresh to God. Often in times of seeking God there is a strong emphasis on repentance, but now I spoke about the positive offering of ourselves to God as instruments of righteousness. After a short time of teaching and explanation, I asked everyone to go away on their own with a piece of paper and do exactly what the Scriptures said. I suggested each person draw a straight line at the top of the paper to represent the whole of their life and then to divide it into sections, each section representing a different area of life.

My own piece of paper looked like this:

| Home | Marriage | Children | Household | Devotional | Ministry | Finance | Emotional | Recreation |

I asked them to take one section at a time and to ask God to show how they could offer it afresh to him and in what ways he by his Spirit wanted to change them and transform each section.

After an hour we all returned and I thought we would probably conclude the morning with a brief time of praise and prayer. What happened took me completely by surprise. This simple exercise had opened hearts in a powerful way, and the next hour and a half were spent in prayer and repentance as God did a further refining work in all our lives.

9

A Man Who Lives to Seek God

I was completely mystified when I first heard of people 'seeking the Lord'. It seemed a good idea and sounded very holy, but what did it mean? To me, it was just a phrase of spiritual jargon. If this chapter is to have any relevance, you need to know what 'seeking God' means.

As a child of God you have been brought from death to life. You have the life of Jesus within you, you have received the Holy Spirit, you are a new creation in Christ. Yet you have not yet obtained all that God has for you, nor have you 'already been made perfect', to quote the apostle Paul (Phil 3:12).

You want to worship God and yet know that you do not worship in the way God desires. You want to be holy and please God and yet know you are not as holy and righteous as he calls you to be. You want a powerful ministry but are only too aware of your limitations. You want to bring only God's word into the lives of others, and yet are conscious of the intrusion of your own wisdom. You want to see only God's kingdom in your ministry, yet you see that other things influence you too. You are surrounded by lost humanity, yet see all too few finding life in Christ.

So what do you do? You seek God!

How do you seek him? The prophet Jeremiah has the answer: 'You will seek me and find me when you seek me with all your heart' (Jer 29:13). In seeking God there is dynamic movement from the unholy towards the holy. It is not a passive exercise: it demands a total giving of yourself to the purposes of God.

A. W. Tozer writes: 'It has been the experience of countless seekers after God that when their desires became a pain they were suddenly and wonderfully filled.'

Breakthrough

As we see ourselves as God sees us, we know that we need a breakthrough! What is a breakthrough? Lovers of cricket will know this word well, for when two batsmen remain hour after hour at the crease during a long hot summer's afternoon, the cry of the fielding side is for a breakthrough, that is, the removal of one of the batsmen. The situation is then changed and the defeat of the batting side is hastened.

As Christians, we can go on in a familiar rut, the same things keep happening day after day and there never seems to be an increase in power. The cry of our hearts is for a breakthrough! A spiritual breakthrough does not happen by accident, but is always deliberately asked for and deeply desired. It means letting go of familiar ways and habits that are comfortable and stepping out in faith into the unknown.

Some questions need answering. Do you want a breakthrough in your life and ministry? If you do, it will cost you something. Are you ready to leave the pathway of past experience and step out into new walks of faith? If you do step out, you will start to become familiar with 'walking on the water'.

A breakthrough begins with a revelation from God, a realization that something needs to change. You can know in your mind that there needs to be a deeper work of God in your life, and you may even try very hard to do something about it. But only God can bring that 'word' into your life that will set into motion the process that leads to a real breakthrough.

When God shows what needs to happen in your life then true repentance is the next step. It is only revelation that leads to repentance. Sin is always at the heart of an inability to move forward in faith. It may be disobedience, impurity or fear; it may be lukewarmness or unbelief. Whatever it is, you need to confess it to God and receive his cleansing.

'Godly sorrow brings repentance that leads to salvation

and leaves no regret' (2 Cor 7:10) is the first principle of breakthrough with God. I have already explained the meaning of true repentance in Chapter 5. Beyond repentance there must be faith and obedience. It is these two factors that bring about the breakthrough. Faith enables you to know that God is able to do something within you and through you that has never happened before. But just knowing is not enough. Obedience gives God the opportunity to do it. Thus there are four simple steps: revelation, repentance, faith, obedience.

Some time ago I was on my way to a weekend of ministry in Wales. I had some other members of the Fellowship with me. As we travelled down the M4 we were praying together. I prayed something like this: 'Father, we believe that people will come into your kingdom tonight, that many will be filled with your Holy Spirit and that your power will be present to bring healing into many lives. Amen.'

Our prayer time continued, but I was left in a state of uncertainty. It had been so easy to speak out those words to God, but I realized I did not have the faith to believe that God would actually do it.

I needed a breakthrough! I knew that God healed, I had no problem with that. I had seen God heal through my own ministry, and yet my faith was at rock bottom. I knew I was afraid to ask people to come forward at the end of the meeting. I thought no one would respond, and if they did I doubted God could use me to be a channel for his healing grace.

'Perhaps that is not my ministry,' I thought, but quickly remembered that the Scriptures promise signs and wonders will follow the preaching of the gospel as a confirmation of its truth. I was trapped both theologically and practically.

We arrived at the church for a time of prayer in preparation for the meeting and I confessed my fear and unbelief to my team. I knew God had been speaking very clearly to me in the car and that I needed to seek him for a new breakthrough in ministry. It was God's word of revelation to my heart that led me to repentance. I needed every minute of that prayer time to seek God and to receive faith for that meeting.

Just before the meeting began I was still struggling with

the fear that nobody would respond to the invitation to come forward when two men came up to inquire whether I would be praying with people at the close of the service, because they had come specifically for prayer. Hallelujah! The Lord was giving me a much needed piece of encouragement. There would be at least two to pray with at the end—I did not dare ask either whether they needed healing!

The church was full, which was also encouraging. There must be some who needed to be healed. My faith was rising.

We had a good meeting. The praise and worship was warm and buoyant and I preached my heart out. As I began the time of ministry, two stood to receive Christ as Saviour and Lord. 'Praise God,' I thought, 'That's the first phrase of the prayer answered'. Many stood to receive the infilling of the Holy Spirit. 'We're on course, Lord. Now here's the crunch!' I then invited people to come to the front to receive prayer for whatever they believed God wanted to give to them, whether it be power, direction, release or healing. I waited expectantly—I knew there would be two!

God's power was at work, and I found myself at the communion rail praying and laying hands on a large number of people. Many testified to an immediate release. A number received the gift of speaking in tongues, others were set free in various ways, and many were prayed with for physical healing. The breakthrough had happened, praise God.

The flatness that often comes at the end of a powerful meeting set in upon me. I had prayed for so many, but had God actually healed anyone? I had been too afraid to ask.

On the following evening I was again praying with people at the end of the meeting and recognized one of those waiting as having been at the front on the previous evening. My thoughts went into negative gear: 'Perhaps it didn't work and he's come back for some more prayer to see whether it will "take" this time.' As I came to him I asked what he wanted to be prayed for.

He answered: 'Nothing. Last night when I came for prayer I had a urinary infection which caused bleeding and which had defied medical cure. After you prayed for me last night I went home and found that the bleeding had stopped. I have come back to give thanks and praise to God. Tomorrow I go to the hospital for what was to be further investigation, but now I can tell them that God has healed me.'

Isn't God loving and gracious? He knew I needed that testimony, and he sent the man back to give it.

A short analysis of the story above shows the principles of breakthrough. After I had prayed in the car God brought real conviction to my heart concerning unbelief. It was a revelation from God and it required my repentance. It did not end there, because the next step was to ask him for a new release of faith, which I did. Faith always needs to be accompanied by obedience. I could have felt full of faith and said to God: 'I will preach the word and then stand back, and you can do the work.' But God's answer to that is: 'You step out in obedience and I will act according to my power and grace.'

I see faith and obedience as two elements that are inseparable. Obedience is my part of the deal, and faith is given by God and releases his power. It is rather like power steering in a car or lorry. When the steering wheel is static, the power mechanism is inoperative. The moment the wheel is turned the power comes into force and all need for human effort and strength is removed. As you step out in obedience, God steps in and does the work.

However, it is not only for breakthrough in power that we need to seek God.

Seeking God for God's sake

For whose sake do you spend time in the presence of God? Most of us would have to admit to a self-centred attitude to time spent with the Lord. But God made us as his creation to worship him and to have fellowship with him for *his* sake. Jesus said: 'Yet a time is coming and has now come when the true worshippers will worship the Father in spirit and truth, for they are the kind of worshippers the Father seeks. God is spirit, and his worshippers must worship in spirit and in truth' (Jn 4:23–24).

I wonder what God thinks of your worship? Does it please him? The Psalms are full of praise to God and they give an insight into the heart of King David who was so eloquent in his expression of worship and love to God. 'I will extol the Lord at all times; his praise will always be on my lips. My soul will boast in the Lord; let the afflicted hear and rejoice. Glorify the Lord with me; let us exalt his name together' (Ps 34:1–3).

Something important happens as time is spent giving to God the glory that is due to his name. God becomes greater to you and his reign is established more firmly in your life. The more you express your love for God, the more love you have for him. The more you worship, the more you want to worship. The more you thank God for all his faithfulness and provision, the more grateful you become for the way he is at work in every detail of your life.

When this happens you begin to identify with the psalmist: 'How lovely is your dwelling-place, O Lord Almighty! My soul yearns, even faints for the courts of the Lord.... Better is one day in your courts than a thousand elsewhere' (Ps 84:1–2, 10).

Supposing I said to you: 'Tomorrow you can spend the whole day with the Lord. Not as a day of prayer and fasting when you are asking God for something, but as a day in which to do nothing else but enjoy his presence.' How would you react? It might be very threatening, as it would be to think of spending time with someone whom you fear or with whom relationship has broken down.

Learn the joy of simply being in the presence of God. 'In thy presence is fulness of joy' (Ps 16:11 AV) says David. Practise the presence of Jesus. In your time with the Lord each day, make room for praise and worship, make room for quietness and allow the joyful presence of the Lord to flow over you like a river of peace.

Why not stop reading now, put this book down and spend some minutes in the presence of the Lord? Tell him that you love and worship him, give him thanks and praise. Tell him that you are enjoying his company and he will tell you that he is enjoying yours.

> One thing I ask of the Lord,
>   this is what I seek:
> that I may dwell in the house of the Lord
>   all the days of my life,
> to gaze upon the beauty of the Lord
>   and to seek him in his temple
>
> (Ps 27:4)

As you learn to seek God for his own glory a few moments at a time, your appetite will grow and you will eventually know that to spend the day with him alone would be sheer joy.

Seeking God for the sake of my life

Time spent in the holy presence of God will always expose sin and lead to repentance (see Chapter 5). This activity can be viewed in two ways—negatively and positively. Both are valid, but one is far more creative than the other.

'Seek the Lord while he may be found; call on him while he is near. Let the wicked forsake his way and the evil man his thoughts (Is 55:6). As we seek God the darkness of our hearts is exposed and we cry out with David: 'Against you, you only, have I sinned' (Ps 51:4). God is gracious and will always forgive and cleanse, and our relationship with him will be restored.

It was during a church weekend at Scunthorpe that God showed me the positive side of seeking him. I was in the middle of speaking on Psalm 51 and expressing the need of repentance for sin, of truth in the inner parts and of being in right relationship with God. Suddenly, verse 10 seemed to leap out of the page towards me: 'Create in me a pure heart, O God.' I had never really understood that verse before. This was not just a casual hope that God would put things right in David's life, but was an impassioned plea for God to do something radical. With the psalmist I cried out to God: 'I want a pure heart, Lord.'

The change was not instant, but it was distinct and it still continues. As the weeks went by, my seeking of God took on a new character. Rather than being centred upon sin and darkness it became focused upon light and holiness. It did not bypass repentance, but gave it a new and positive dynamic.

Isaiah says: 'Seek the Lord and you will become aware of the need to forsake sin' (my paraphrase of Is 55:6). The prophet Amos advises: 'Seek the Lord and live' (Amos 5:6). It is not only a matter of climbing out of defeat but of stepping into victory!

There is a familiar verse in James 4:7—'Resist the devil, and he will flee from you.' Many try to do that and fail. The reason is that they forget the first sentence of that verse: 'Submit yourselves, then, to God.' The positive submission of our lives to God releases the power and faith to resist the devil and extinguish all his flaming arrows. My experience of positively seeking God for my life gave a new meaning to that verse in Philippians 4:8—'Finally, brothers, whatever is true, whatever is noble, whatever is right, whatever is pure, whatever is lovely, whatever is admirable—if anything is excellent or praiseworthy—think about such things.'

Seeking God for power in ministry

The breakthrough in faith for healing that God gave me in Wales illustrates the way he releases his power in response to faith. But a triumph of faith one weekend does not make faith any easier the next! The exercise of seeking God for his power in ministry is a daily one. Even though confidence in God is strengthened, the fact that I always need to step out in faith is the constant reality of 'walking on the water'.

The Scriptures clearly say: 'And without faith it is impossible to please God, because anyone who comes to him must believe that he exists and that he rewards those who earnestly seek him' (Heb 11:6). I find that verse very uncomfortable. My human nature would like to be able to gather experience in ministry so that I could be sure that everything I did would work. But the Holy Spirit teaches me that I need to operate in faith at all times.

I know I have no power, humanly speaking, to convert any person to Christ or to give anyone power for living or to administer any healing. It is God alone who does these things, and he uses frail human instruments filled with his power to do his work. I am fully aware that I can do no miracles myself, but I am also aware of the awesome responsibility placed upon me by God that he wants to do miracles through me (Heb 2:3–4).

To seek God for power in ministry is to acknowledge before him in humility my own lack of power, and to ask him to pour through me his majesty and strength. Then his work will not be hampered by my lack of faith.

In Mark 9 there is the incident of the boy with the evil spirit whom the disciples failed to release and whom Jesus subsequently set free. That failure caused some deep questioning among the disciples: '"Why couldn't we drive it out?" [Jesus] replied, "This kind can come out only by prayer"' (Mk 9:28–29).

God's power was not in question. There was nothing lacking in God's ability to set the boy free. So the conclusion must be that there was a paucity of prayer among the disciples. God needed to deal with unbelief, perhaps pride or self-sufficiency, so that the disciples could be used for his finest purposes.

Prayer and seeking God change you so that God can work more freely through you. Acts 3 is a superb sequel to the failure of Mark 9, as Peter and John were used by God to perform a miracle in the life of the lame man. God had not changed, nor had the circumstances, but something had definitely changed in the lives of Peter and John.

I live with that dynamic tension in my own life. I know that nothing is too difficult for God and I want to see his power at work in those to whom I minister. I see him do many powerful and gracious things, yet I am always conscious that more could happen. That is what keeps me seeking God.

Time and again during a Leaders' Week at The Hyde, as I meet with the team for prayer, we will look at one another and say: 'We need a breakthrough!' That is when the talking ends and the praying begins. We cry out to God: 'Lord, come among us in your mighty power and meet with us.' As we pray God deals with us and continues to do so as we go into the meeting. We are overwhelmed with gratitude as we see God at work transforming our lives, and the lives of those who are with us, by cleansing, healing and empowering.

Complacency is the greatest enemy of spiritual strength. It is true that as we grow in faith and authority, we learn to have a greater confidence in God. And yet there is always more. So with Paul we need to say: 'Forgetting what is behind and straining towards what is ahead, I press on towards the goal to win the prize for which God has called me heavenwards in Christ Jesus' (Phil 3:13–14).

Seeking God for the right message for the people

Those whose calling is preaching and teaching know that all Scripture is God-breathed and profitable and will therefore benefit the hearers. Though that is true, it is inspiration from God that will show which part, or parts, of the Scriptures he wishes to be brought before the people at any particular time, and what message is to be given.

As a preacher you have the responsibility before God to hear from him the right word for each situation, and that will entail seeking God.

I have outlined how to hear the voice of God for yourself (Chapter 7) but now you have to put that into practice with regard to receiving a message that others need to hear.

Some of you may be teaching by going consecutively through a book of the Bible. That is good, but it is not a substitute for today's word from God which addresses today's need.

There is a song that says:

> We need to hear from you
> We need a word from you
> If we don't hear from you
> What will we do?

The right word for God's people will break open situations that have become seemingly immovable, it will lead them on into maturity and faith and will challenge commitment and lead to greater obedience and discipleship.

It is important to guard against the message being a reactive one, born out of need and frustration. It must be a creative word that comes from the heart of God. Then it will reach right into the hearts of the people.

How do you seek God for the right word? I cannot give any quick answers. You need to live in the word of God as Paul advises the Colossians: 'Let the word of Christ dwell in you richly as you teach and admonish one another with all wisdom' (Col 3:16). In Jeremiah there is a similar promise: 'But if they had stood in my council, they would have proclaimed my words to my people' (Jer 23:22).

Time needs to be given to waiting before God quietly in prayer. I find that during times like this God's prayer language—speaking in tongues—is of great value. As I pray to him in the language he has given me, I find that he speaks into my heart the words he wants his people to hear.

You also need to be open to God giving you something new at the last moment. A too tightly prepared message often leaves little room for God to break through with the unexpected. If you leave room for God you will find he will say things through you that are as much a surprise to you as they are to those listening to you. That deals with any pride there may be, as you know without a doubt that it was not your idea, but his!

Having received a word from the Lord, how it is prepared for delivery will vary from one person to another. This is not a book about homiletics! So all I say to you is: give time to seeking God for his prophetic word to his people; you will find it life-changing and so will they.

Seeking God on behalf of others

As a leader or minister you will often be called upon to give help to individuals; there will be a constant flow of people coming to your door needing spiritual assistance in one way or another. Your need to see God's power at work in these situations will again lead you to seek him.

Human wisdom and counselling techniques have their uses, but they are limited. Good advice has never transformed a life that is under the domination of the kingdom of darkness. Only God can do that. You need to understand that every problem is basically a spiritual one.

Therefore seeking God on behalf of others works in two directions. First, when I am confronted with someone needing help, I will seek God to give me faith for that particular need. It does not matter whether I am aware of the problem or totally ignorant of it. I will spend time with God to allow him to speak words of faith into my heart so that I go into the situation full of faith.

To give a simple illustration: someone is coming to me to receive the baptism in the Holy Spirit. I prepare my heart beforehand so that I receive confidence from the word of God that what I ask for in his name he will do (Mk 11:24).

The Bible says: 'For John baptised with water, but in a few days you will be baptised with the Holy Spirit' (Acts 1:5). Jesus also said: 'For everyone who asks receives' (Lk 11:10) and 'But you will receive power when the Holy Spirit comes on you' (Acts 1:8). Before I begin to minister I need to allow those words to release faith in my own heart. They will then be able to liberate faith in the heart of the person with whom I am praying.

Those Scriptures have become life and power to me and because I know they are God's living word, I also know that as the person for whom I am praying receives them he too will be filled with the Holy Spirit.

Let me confess that there was a time in my life when my confidence in God to meet with anyone through me was very shaky. But I am learning to seek God for his authority in ministry and, although I still feel a great sense of inadequacy, I am learning to trust his faithfulness.

'So then faith cometh by hearing, and hearing by the word of God' (Rom 10:17 AV). As the person with whom I am praying simply asks God to fill him with the power of the Holy Spirit, I know that God will do it, as promised in the

Bible.

Being filled with the Spirit is not tested by feelings, nor by some outward manifestation of a spiritual gift. These things may be given but they are not essential proof that the prayer has worked.

According to God's word, that person has asked so he has received. He is now baptized with the Holy Spirit and has received power. I will encourage him to give thanks to God, and I know that as he continues in thanksgiving he will receive all the assurance he needs. I will tell him that he can now expect to receive spiritual gifts—particularly a prayer language from God—and that he will know a new joy and power in his life. Why? Because he has some wonderful feeling? No, because it is God's promise.

Therefore, the first direction of seeking God is to ask for his faith and thus receive his confidence. 'Such confidence as this is ours through Christ before God. Not that we are competent to claim anything for ourselves, but our competence comes from God' (2 Cor 3:4–5).

The second direction of seeking God is for revelation concerning the situation ahead. I have just described a straightforward situation with which you will probably be familiar. The need is known and the scriptural promises are clear.

Often the need is less clearly defined and more complex. In that case, having gained faith and confidence before God, I proceed to seek him for revelation. I may receive a scripture or an indication of the way to proceed. Or I may simply have the assurance that God is in control and will reveal things as necessary. Here I must cultivate the habit of listening with spiritual ears and stop listening with natural ears. 'But the natural man receiveth not the things of the Spirit of God' (1 Cor 2:14 AV).

This is where the gifts of the Holy Spirit become important. I expect God to reveal whatever is necessary through a word of knowledge; to release his power through a gift of faith, healing or a miracle; and to confirm the ministry by a prophetic word or picture and through the Scriptures.

I now expect God to give a prophetic word every time I minister to someone and he never lets me down. Faith is not based on powerful prayer, or on the laying on of hands, but on the word of God.

Seeking God on behalf of the lost

No one ever became a Christian because they thought it was a good idea. Lost mankind does not seek after God. It was God's idea that brought you to himself, not yours. You may find that difficult to believe when you think back to those years of searching, but actually the searching arose because God was looking for you and thus his Spirit created an unrest within you that only God could satisfy. Jesus said: 'No-one can come to me unless the Father who sent me draws him' (Jn 6:44).

So the lost do not search for God. God calls his people to seek him on behalf of the lost. The great commission is: 'go and make disciples of all nations' (Mt 28:19) and that call is as strong today as the day it was first spoken. It means not only preaching the gospel, but giving time to seeking God with sacrificial intercessory prayer.

True intercession is costly because it means to stand before God on behalf of another. That most familiar of all Bible texts says: 'For God so loved the world that he gave his one and only Son' (Jn 3:16). God's love involved action: he gave Jesus to die on a cross for our sins. It says prophetically of Jesus in Isaiah: 'For he bore the sin of many, and made intercession for the transgressors' (Is 53:12).

So seeking God on behalf of the lost involves asking him for his love for them. This is not a vague request but will be centred on certain individuals. This will mean asking God how to pray for that person, then making a commitment to prayer and obedience in action until either the prayer burden lifts or the person comes through to faith. The promise of God's word is: 'The prayer of a righteous man is powerful and effective' (Jas 5:16).

I have a good friend, Bob Hamblin, who became a Christian when he was 40 years old. He had been a blasphemer and led a thoroughly godless life. During his late twenties he had travelled to London daily by train and taken a certain amount of pleasure in poking fun at a fellow commuter who was a Christian. When eventually Bob came to faith in Christ, he remembered this man and the ridicule he had poured out on him and felt that he must find him to share the good news and apologize for the way he had persecuted him for his faith. Bob found out where the man lived and went to visit him. Great joy was shared and forgiveness was asked for and received. However, the most interesting thing that Bob's friend said was this: 'Now I know that eleven years of prayer were not wasted.' Praise God for those who will intercede on behalf of the lost.

Seeking God is a process of recognizing need, acknowledging sin and failure and reaching out to the living God. God will then meet the need, forgive the sin and failure and pour out his life and power. As you seek God, self-centredness is transformed into Christ-centredness. Unholiness and impurity is admitted and you cry out: 'Create in me a pure heart, O God.'

Weakness and ineffectiveness is acknowledged and opens up the way for you to receive the power of the living God; unbelief is transformed into faith; human wisdom is exchanged for God's revelation; the kingdom of darkness is defeated by the kingdom of heaven; and indifference towards lost mankind is changed into a passion for souls.

'But if from there you seek the Lord your God, you will find him if you look for him with all your heart and with all your soul' (Deut 4:29).

PART 2

The Principles of a Leader's Work

10

A Man of the Gospel

'How long have you been a Christian?' I asked.

'Well, I was brought up to go to church, but I did not really become committed to the church until I joined the youth group as a teenager. Later on I became an active member of the church council and have since had responsibility in many areas of church life', was the reply.

'When did Jesus Christ first become real to you?' I asked next.

'My parents brought me up to go to church and our family has been religious as long as I can remember,' he said.

'You haven't answered my question,' I probed further. 'I am asking you if you have entered into the reality of a personal relationship with Jesus Christ as Lord?'

'I am a church member', came back the somewhat puzzled response.

'Have you ever been to the cross?'

'No.'

'That is what needs to happen now,' I said.

This was the gist of the conversation that I had with Geoff, who had come to see me at his own request because of a long-standing condition of depression. He had been referred to the Bethany Fellowship by his minister.

What I discovered was that although many people had prayed with him about the depression, no one had questioned whether he had a basic relationship with Jesus Christ. That question about the cross revealed that Geoff was not 'born again' of the Holy Spirit. As Paul said to the Romans: 'And if anyone does not have the Spirit of Christ, he does not belong to Christ' (Rom 8:9).

I simply led Geoff in a prayer of repentance as together we came to the cross of Jesus. All the sin, failure, shattered hopes, fears and disappointment were brought to the loving Saviour. I spoke out to him the promise of forgiveness that follows true confession in 1 John 1:9: 'If we confess our sins, he is faithful and just and will forgive us our sins and purify us from all unrighteousness.'

Geoff then offered his life to God and asked for his salvation. As we prayed together Geoff became a new creation in Christ, the old passed away, the new arrived! (2 Cor 5:17.) I prayed further with him and God graciously filled him with his Holy Spirit.

As the time of prayer concluded, I looked at Geoff and the transformation that had taken place was remarkable—so much so, that I completely forgot to pray about the depression. The fact was that the releasing work of the cross had dispelled the heaviness and depression. Geoff was free and rejoicing in his new life in Jesus.

Paul said in Romans 1:16: 'I am not ashamed of the gospel, because it is the power of God for the salvation of everyone who believes.' The gospel is the bedrock of all ministry. Every person needs to hear and receive the life-transforming gospel message. What then is the gospel? It simply means 'good news', the joyful message that 'Christ Jesus came into the world to save sinners' (1 Tim 1:15). As it says in Mark 1:14–15, 'Jesus went into Galilee, proclaiming the good news of God. "The time has come," he said. "The kingdom of God is near. Repent and believe the good news!"'

The gospel is much more than simply the message of salvation to sinners, but unless it includes that fundamental message it is not the gospel. There is a danger today with all kinds of new emphases that a 'minister of the gospel' will fail to bring that vital message which leads people to personal salvation.

There is absolutely no value in teaching about the fullness of the Holy Spirit, physical or emotional healing, the needs of the Third World, the Christian life or prayer counselling if a person has not passed from death to life; from darkness to light.

You may wonder why I am expressing this so strongly. In the Bethany Fellowship we receive an enormous number of requests from churches and individuals for prayer and counselling. There is a constant stream of people who come with physical and emotional needs, who are then ministered to by a pastoral team. It is amazing the number of times that the blockage preventing healing for many years has been that the person has never committed his or her life to Christ, nor received forgiveness and salvation.

Although you will meet people who have received healing without becoming Christians, healing that does not lead to discipleship does not bring wholeness. Therefore the first priority of ministry is to preach the gospel and lead people to saving faith in Christ. In order to do this with assurance and confidence, the principles involved need to be clearly grasped.

The truth of man's condition

Before you can declare the good news of the gospel, you need to tell people the bad news of the consequences of sin and lives that are without Christ. I do not think 'hellfire' preaching is too popular these days, but it is all too easy to minimize the consequences of sin and therefore diminish the dynamic of the gospel message.

The fact is that God is holy and natural mankind is unholy. As you walk through your home town, how do you view the people who surround you? Are they just faceless masses? Or are they those for whom Christ died? I find the familiarity of those whom I constantly meet dulls my sensitivity to their plight without Christ.

Several months ago when taking a church weekend in the north of England, I found walking through Newcastle on a Saturday afternoon to be a very challenging exercise. The sadness and sense of loss on the faces of the shoppers struck me powerfully. I had to confess that the faces of people in Crawley (our local town) were no different, but I had not been so aware of their need. Paul described such people as: 'without hope and without God in the world' (Eph 2:12).

The words 'for all have sinned and fall short of the glory of

God' (Rom 3:23) are so familiar, but do we live in the consciousness that those who remain that way are living in peril of eternal death and separation from God?

Jesus was criticized for the company he kept. He avoided the respectable and religious people and gave his time to the disreputable. The final statement he spoke to Zacchaeus states clearly the purpose of his ministry: 'For the Son of Man came to seek and to save what was lost' (Lk 19:10).

Mankind needs to know its lostness without Christ and your preaching about the bad news needs to be as strong as it is about the good news.

The universality of God's love

God's love is at the heart of the gospel message. Probably the best-known words in the whole Bible are: 'For God so loved the world that he gave his one and only Son, that whoever believes in him shall not perish but have eternal life' (Jn 3:16).

Because God is holy and righteous he cannot accept fallen mankind into his holy presence. However, he longs to have the relationship of 'a father with his children' with his own creation. He does not want his own children to perish, which is the consequence of their sin and rebellion. So, God has taken the initiative in sending his Son, Jesus Christ, to pay the ultimate sacrifice of his own life to bring mankind back into relationship with himself. Why? Because God knows the righteous judgement for sin, but 'wants all men to be saved and to come to a knowledge of the truth' (1 Tim 2:4).

God has chosen to use his own people to bring his vital message to lost mankind. Jesus sent his disciples out, saying: 'Go into all the world and preach the good news to all creation' (Mk 16:15). God has poured out his love into your heart by the Holy Spirit (Rom 5:5) so that you can pour out his love to lost humanity by bringing them the good news of sins forgiven and new life in Christ.

The salvation of God is unique

The gospel knows of only one way for man to be made right with God. 'Salvation is found in no-one else, for there is no other name under heaven given to men by which we must be saved' (Acts 4:12).

There is nothing that man can do; religious observance and good deeds cannot earn him salvation, nor can righteous living and kindness to others. God's unique way of salvation is by grace alone.

Paul's letter to the Ephesians tells us: 'For it is by grace you have been saved, through faith—and this not from yourselves, it is the gift of God—not by works, so that no-one can boast' (Eph 2:8–9).

The simplicity of man's response

In that famous sermon on the day of Pentecost when the Holy Spirit fell on the first disciples, Peter declared: 'And everyone who calls on the name of the Lord will be saved' (Acts 2:21). As the good news is declared in simplicity and power it calls for a response. Those who heard Peter's sermon said: '"Brothers, what shall we do?" Peter replied, "Repent and be baptised, every one of you, in the name of Jesus Christ so that your sins may be forgiven. And you will receive the gift of the Holy Spirit"' (Acts 2:37–38).

It is repentance and faith that lead to salvation. It is not sufficient to hear the message or even to hear and to agree, 'For we also have had the gospel preached to us, just as they did; but the message they heard was of no value to them, because those who heard did not combine it with faith' (Heb 4:2).

The gospel is so simple that it is an offence to many who would like an intellectual ideology. The truth is that God has made salvation the simplest thing in the world, and yet the knowledge of God will occupy all our mind and strength for an entire lifespan without our ever coming near to full understanding.

'Jews demand miraculous signs and Greeks look for

wisdom, but we preach Christ crucified: a stumbling block to Jews and foolishness to Gentiles, but to those whom God has called, both Jews and Greeks, Christ the power of God and the wisdom of God' (1 Cor 1:22–24).

The good news of God carries transforming power

In spite of its simplicity the good news works a miracle in the life of the believer. In fact it is the greatest supernatural act that can happen to anyone. Paul said to the Corinthians: 'Therefore, if anyone is in Christ, he is a new creation; the old has gone, the new has come!' (2 Cor 5:17.)

It is impossible for someone to have received new life in Christ and not to know it. For some it is as dramatic as it was for Saul of Tarsus on the Damascus Road, for others it happens quietly, perhaps alone in prayer to God. However, the fact that it has happened will be distinct and measurable.

There will be an assurance of forgiveness and cleansing. 'In him we have redemption through his blood, the forgiveness of sins' (Eph 1:7).

The turmoil of life, and guilt caused by sin, will have yielded to God's peace. 'Therefore, since we have been justified through faith, we have peace with God through our Lord Jesus Christ' (Rom 5:1).

The power of sin will have been broken and there will be a knowledge of victory. This will already have happened in some areas of life and the fact that it can happen in every area will have been understood. 'For sin shall not be your master, because you are not under law, but under grace' (Rom 6:14).

The reality of God's presence

We have looked at the basic ingredients of the gospel message. Now how do we know that a person is a child of God? It is not because they responded at a certain evangelistic meeting; it is not because they were baptized or confirmed at some time or other; it is not because they are a church member and faithful supporter of all its activities. It is because Christ lives in them today by the power of his Holy Spirit.

There is a story told of a man who had a remarkable conversion experience, and was in great demand to give his testimony. Not being a particularly able speaker, he had written down all the details on a piece of paper. The precious document was kept in a drawer. Every time an invitation came for him to speak, the paper was carefully removed and the testimony given. This went on for a number of years. However, one day when an invitation arrived, he went to the drawer as usual and discovered that the 'testimony' had been eaten by mice. The man was horrified and, making contact with the organizer, said: 'I am sorry, I cannot speak at your meeting. I am afraid mice have eaten my testimony!'

The reality of God's salvation cannot be eaten by mice. There is a ring of confidence in the testimony of all who know the reality of God's presence. The apostle Paul wrote to Timothy: 'I know whom I have believed' (2 Tim 1:12). And John in his first letter says: 'We know that we live in him and he in us, because he has given us of his Spirit' (1 Jn 4:13).

The priority of the gospel in ministry

As one who ministers, what priority does the gospel message have in your preaching? Do you know which people in your congregation or group have received the life of Jesus? If not, you need to.

God has a purpose for all his children, which is to become like his Son Jesus, to become mature, attaining to the whole measure of the fullness of God (Eph 4:13). Spiritual growth cannot happen in people who have not received spiritual life.

Even though Paul has given us a tremendous depth of spiritual teaching, his commitment to the simple gospel never wavered. 'Woe to me if I do not preach the gospel!' he said to the Corinthians (1 Cor 9:16). 'I have become all things to all men so that by all possible means I might save some' (v.22).

Paul asked the Ephesians to pray that God would give him greater boldness: 'Pray also for me, that whenever I open my mouth, words may be given me so that I will fearlessly make known the mystery of the gospel' (Eph 6:19).

The gospel message will always create opposition in those

who do not want to leave their old way of life. Yet that was no deterrent to Paul, because he knew the consequences of sin and realized how near he himself came to going to a lost eternity. He considered that suffering for the gospel was a privilege, and would stop at nothing in order to rescue the lost. 'We had previously suffered and been insulted in Philippi, as you know, but with the help of our God we dared to tell you his gospel in spite of strong opposition' (1 Thess 2:2).

A man of the gospel will fearlessly declare that life-changing message. However, no man ever transformed the people in his church merely from the pulpit. Having spoken the truth with clarity and boldness, he needs to find out person by person where each one is in relation to God, and lead them through to personal faith. That is not to say that the pastor or minister will personally lead all of them to Christ, but he will know that each person has been confronted with the gospel, and that each one who has responded has been led to repentance and received the assurance of sins forgiven.

I have often been asked by ministers who are moving to a new church where they should start. My reply is always: 'Start by making sure that every person in your church has a living faith in Christ.' Without the foundation of vital personal faith you cannot develop true discipleship and lead your people to know and experience the life and power of the Holy Spirit.

My uncle, who lives in California, once described the majority of those who attend his church as 'the living dead'. If you confirm people whom Christ has not converted, or admit into church membership those who have not entered the kingdom of God, you are inviting trouble.

Leading people to Christ

It is surprising how many leaders and ministers lack confidence in leading individuals to personal faith in Christ. This has been my own experience. Despite having gone through various Christian life and witness courses, going right back to the early visits of Billy Graham, I was totally lacking in confidence when it came to leading a person to Christ. For years I organized Youth for Christ meetings in our town, and month by month evangelists would come and preach the gospel and invite the unconverted to yield their lives to Jesus. At the time of the invitation I would be in great conflict; I sincerely wanted people to commit their lives to Christ and yet was afraid that any individuals I might pray with would not really come to a living faith in him. Therefore, I hardly knew how to pray. If I asked God for a big response, then my secret fear of having to pray with someone would come to pass, and if no one came forward the whole exercise would seem to be a disappointment and a failure. I am thankful that there was a good response over the years and many found living faith in Christ. However, my own personal conflict remained.

It has only been more recently that I have found that confidence in God, and now if someone asks me to pray with them for salvation I can respond with joy and not fear. I know that one of the things that has strengthened my confidence has been to lead people through distinct steps when bringing them to salvation.

Steps that lead to faith in Christ

1. Salvation takes place at the cross of Jesus

The salvation of God takes place at the cross of Jesus. That is where Jesus died, shed his blood and purchased redemption for mankind. Help a person to picture himself coming to the cross, where sin is dealt with, where the past can be left behind, where fear and doubt can disappear and where all things become new.

2. Salvation begins with repentance

If there is time, and always in an ongoing pastoral situation, ask the person to have their repentance prepared and written down in detail. In the Fellowship we often call this 'writing a letter to Jesus'. It is important not only to write down sin, failure, fears and doubts, but also the positive side; that is, to offer oneself to God, and to yield to God your relationships, marriage, family, home, work, time, money and possessions.

Ask him (or her!) to pray this out to God in your presence. 'For it is with your heart that you believe and are justified, and it is with your mouth that you confess and are saved' (Rom 10:10).

3. Salvation leads to forgiveness, cleansing and freedom

After the prayer of repentance, thank God for sins forgiven and read out confirmatory scriptures:

'If we confess our sins, he is faithful and just and will forgive us our sins and purify us from all unrighteousness' (1 Jn 1:9).

'Therefore, there is now no condemnation for those who are in Christ Jesus' (Rom 8:1).

'Godly sorrow brings repentance that leads to salvation and leaves no regret' (2 Cor 7:10).

'It is for freedom that Christ has set us free. Stand firm, then, and do not not let yourselves be burdened again by a yoke of slavery' (Gal 5:1).

4. The life of Jesus comes in

At this point, ask the person to pray a simple prayer giving the whole of his life over to God, relinquishing the sovereignty of self and yielding to the will of God. The fact is that the new life in Christ is a change of ownership, and true discipleship means to forsake one's own way and to go God's way. Lay your hands on the person and declare the promises of God: 'You have given to God your old life full of sin, failure and defeat. Now, God has given you his life, you are cleansed by the blood of Jesus, you can now live the resurrection life of Jesus because when he arose he defeated sin and death and paved the way for the new life you now have.'

5. Power is needed to live the new life

God has given the person his new life, but that life can only be lived in God's divine strength and not by human effort. Get the person to ask God to fill him with his Holy Spirit so that he will have power in his new-found life in Christ.

After he has prayed, again lay your hand on his head and

thank God that according to his word: 'everyone who asks receives' (Lk 11:10). God is now filling him with all his power: 'you will receive power when the Holy Spirit comes on you' (Acts 1:8).

Encourage him to expect God to release the gifts of the Holy Spirit into his life and in particular the prayer language of the Holy Spirit (speaking in tongues). This will sometimes happen spontaneously during prayer, but often it occurs later during the times of thanksgiving that follow.

6. Declare the truth of what God has done

It is important to declare the truth of what God has done in the person's life. Speak this out to him, or lead him to say faith-building statements after you that will bring assurance. For example: 'God is my Father, Jesus is my Saviour, I am a son of God, I am forgiven, I am cleansed, I am a new creation. The past has gone, I am filled with the power of the Holy Spirit, I am now a follower of Jesus, and I love him.'

'Jesus said, "If you hold to my teaching, you are really my disciples. Then you will know the truth, and the truth will set you free"' (Jn 8:31–32).

7. Finish with thanksgiving and praise

There are times when the person will feel nothing. That is not important. New life in Jesus is not a feeling, it is a fact. Now encourage him to thank and praise God for what he has done. Continue to encourage him to go on thanking and praising God, particularly during the first few hours and days. There is real victory in praise.

If anyone has in sincerity followed these simple steps of faith, they will certainly have found new life in Jesus, and will know it!

Finally, we must never lose sight of the simplicity of the gospel, for when anyone calls out in simple faith to God, he is more than ready to respond.

In the moment of crisis, when the earthquake in Philippi had burst the prison open, the jailer, fearing that all the prisoners might have escaped, cried out: 'Men, what must I do to be saved?'

He may have been asking how he might escape execution at the hand of the Romans, but Paul and Silas answered the deeper question that was of far greater importance: 'Believe in the Lord Jesus, and you will be saved—you and your household.'

They looked at Jesus, received his life and were filled with joy because they had come to believe in God (Acts 16:25–34).

II

A Man of the Spirit

For me it all began with a Bible that was held together with red sticky tape. The Bible belonged to my sister Carolyn who had just returned from college in Cheltenham with the news that she had been filled with the Holy Spirit. There was no doubt that something had happened to her—she had a new sense of joy and peace and shared with me her fresh love for God's word. She also said that she now prayed in tongues, which did not impress me one bit.

But my theology was challenged. I had been taught that I had received everything at conversion, and so my response to Carolyn was warm but defensive.

'I am really glad that you have had this new experience of God,' I said, 'but I don't believe I need such an experience in order to draw closer to God or to know more of his power.' Carolyn's reaction was gracious and loving; she did not try to change my mind, but her new enthusiasm for Jesus just kept tumbling out.

The youth fellowship, which was held in part of our home, was going really well. Over the previous five years we had seen it grow from twenty-five to well in excess of 150. Young people were becoming Christians almost every week and we had a large number coming from the fifth and sixth forms of both boys' and girls' grammar schools. In fact you might say I was in the middle of a real success story, but something nagged away inside me and I knew there was a real lack in my Christian life.

Every time Carolyn returned home from college there was that tattered Bible stuck together with more and more red sticky tape. And yet my own Bible was suffering from neglect rather than over-use.

Carolyn and Joyce were getting their heads together, and Joyce seemed quite enthusiastic herself to know this new power of the Holy Spirit. I dug in my heels and determined that I would get through in my own way

At about this time I kept meeting people in whom I recognized a really close walk with God. When I began to talk to them in greater detail, I found that each one could point back to a time when they had been filled, or baptized, with the Holy Spirit.

The success of the youth fellowship continued, but I knew in my heart that I had taken the youngsters as far as I could. I remember one night kneeling down beside my bed feeling deeply discouraged by the emptiness of my own walk with God. 'Lord,' I said, 'I have nothing more to give to these kids unless you do something new in me.'

God seemed to be closing in on me. Joyce and I had become friendly with the new curate of Camborne, Barry Kissell, and his wife Mary. Here again were people who had that special something about them. I did not bother to ask what it was—I knew what the answer would be!

Barry and some of his friends had organized a young people's holiday in Northern Ireland and had persuaded Joyce, myself and a few of our young people to join them.

Carolyn managed to get in on the act too, and so it was that we set off in my car with six-month-old Daniel in a carrycot in the back. Friends had kindly agreed to care for our two older children, Craig and Joanna.

Throughout the journey Carolyn and Joyce were in deep discussion about this infilling of the Holy Spirit. How does it happen? What is the effect? By this time I was thoroughly bored with the whole subject. Nearly two years had elapsed since Carolyn had brought this thing to my notice. The cry of my heart now was: 'Lord, please, let it happen, or let it go away and never be spoken of again.'

The first few days of the holiday reassured me. No one tried to buttonhole me in order to lay hands on me, and for a while I thought it might all subside and be forgotten. And yet my feelings were not of relief but of potential disappointment, for I knew of the emptiness and powerlessness of my relationship with God.

Things began to happen one day as we were sitting together in the quiet room of the conference centre. Joyce innocently turned to Barry and said: 'Would you tell us how you were filled with the Holy Spirit?' And so, in an entirely unemotional way, Barry unfolded the story of how God had met with him. As he finished, Joyce calmly spoke out again: 'Would you pray with *us* to be filled with the Spirit?' She had not asked me whether I wanted to be included in the *us*!

Barry could see the surprise written all over my face, so he asked: 'Charles, do you want me to pray with you.' My surprise quickly changed to relief as I replied: 'Yes, I would like you to.'

Barry explained that to receive the infilling of the Holy Spirit was as simple as receiving Christ as Saviour. You simply had to ask, to receive by faith and to thank God for fulfilling his promise.

Joyce was prayed for first and Barry asked me to join with him in laying on hands. Nothing spectacular occurred, there was just a tremendous sense of the peace and presence of Jesus. Joyce then joined Barry to lay hands on me and to pray. At that moment I felt nothing, I simply received by faith and gladly spoke out my thanks to God. I was relieved there had been no fireworks, and glad it had happened. But what in fact had happened?

By the time we reached our bedroom we both knew that something important had taken place. There was a deep sense of the presence of God and a joy I had not known before. There had been times after a stirring meeting when I had felt inspired and resolved to follow God more closely, but by the morning my feelings had gone and my resolve had evaporated. How would I now feel in the morning?

When I awoke I knew that God's Holy Spirit had done something in me that could not be removed by sleep or time. I had walked through a doorway into a deeper understanding of God.

As my hunger for God's word grew, as it had done for Carolyn, I saw how clearly it taught the need to be filled with the Holy Spirit. How blind I had been! I realized that it was not sufficient just to be a man of the gospel: I also needed to be a man of the Spirit.

Be filled with the Spirit

I could now see how my traditional beliefs had emphasized justification by faith, but it had seemed that subsequent progress in the Christian life had to be by human effort. How I had tried to be a powerful Christian! I also saw how I had limited the power of God and lived such a defeated life. I now wanted to lead others to know the same power and joy I had just received.

If a leader wants my advice about where to lead his people next, I will first ask: 'Do all of your people have a personal faith in Christ?' If the answer is affirmative my next question will be: 'Are they all filled with the Holy Spirit?'

To be filled with the Holy Spirit is not some five-star Christian experience that is reserved for the few. It is a vital *basic* necessity for all believers. It does not indicate spiritual maturity, but is essential for all who want to become mature in Christ. It does not need to take many years of seeking, but can and should be received at the same time as the new birth.

Jesus forbade his disciples even to start the work to which he had called them until they had received the power of the Holy Spirit. 'I am going to send you what my Father has promised; but stay in the city until you have been clothed with power from on high' (Lk 24:49). Despite three years of careful training by Jesus himself, the disciples were still not equipped for the task of spreading the life-changing message of the gospel.

It is so important for all Christians, and especially leaders, to grasp the fact that humanly speaking there is absolutely nothing you can do to please God or to change anyone. Jesus said: 'apart from me you can do nothing' (Jn 15:5). This may not please your ego too much, but unless it is clearly understood you will try to exercise your leadership in human strength and not by God's power.

Paul said: 'Do not get drunk on wine, which leads to debauchery. Instead, be filled with the Spirit' (Eph 5:18).

Here he is contrasting two kinds of power, that of alcohol and that of the Spirit. The one leads to sin and the other brings glory to God.

Again Paul contrasted human wisdom with the power of God: 'My message and my preaching were not with wise and persuasive words, but with a demonstration of the Spirit's power, so that your faith might not rest on men's wisdom, but on God's power' (1 Cor 2:4–5).

Being filled with the Holy Spirit is not a once-only experience. When Paul commands: 'Be filled with the Spirit' he is speaking in the present continuous tense which gives the meaning 'go on being filled with the Spirit'. D. L. Moody once said: 'I am filled with the Holy Spirit, but I leak.'

The disciples in Acts 2 were all filled with the Holy Spirit on the Day of Pentecost. That initial infilling is referred to by Jesus in Acts 1:5—'For John baptised with water, but in a few days you will be baptised with the Holy Spirit.' Yet in Acts 4:31 we discover that following their prayer for more boldness: 'they were all filled with the Holy Spirit'.

Therefore as a leader you need first to bring your people to know Holy Spirit baptism for themselves and the power that he gives, but you also need to keep your people living in daily dependence upon the strength of the Spirit. 'If we live in the Spirit, let us also walk in the Spirit' (Gal 5:25 AV).

The Holy Spirit produces fruit to the glory of God

Human life was never intended by God to be lived out in human strength. In fact God knew that under the pressure of temptation our humanity would soon crumble. He therefore provided his power so that we could live lives that would bring glory to him.

So Paul wrote: 'So I say, live by the Spirit, and you will not gratify the desires of the sinful nature' (Gal 5:16). The Holy Spirit will touch every area of your life, giving power in service and ministry, and a transformation in lifestyle and attitudes. 'But the fruit of the Spirit is love, joy, peace, patience, kindness, goodness, faithfulness, gentleness and self-control. Against such things there is no law' (Gal 5:

22–23). (I have dealt with this subject in detail in Chapter 8.)

The Holy Spirit releases gifts for life and ministry

Although I did not speak in tongues at the time when I was baptized with the Holy Spirit, once having entered the realm of the Spirit I soon desired to receive everything God had for me. The Scriptures say: 'He who speaks in a tongue edifies himself' (1 Cor 14:4) and I knew that I needed to be built up in the life of the Spirit. It was not long before I was on Barry's doorstep asking him to pray that I might receive the gift of speaking in tongues. I began, very falteringly, but soon I was entering into the truth of God's word and being strengthened in my prayer life by this gift from God.

Paul said: 'Follow the way of love and eagerly desire spiritual gifts, especially the gift of prophecy' (1 Cor 14:1). The gifts of the Spirit are so necessary in today's church and should be central to its life and worship, not hidden away in the Wednesday night prayer group.

The voice of God must be heard: 'no-one knows the thoughts of God except the Spirit of God' (1 Cor 2:11). Therefore, gifts of prophecy and words of wisdom and knowledge need to be received from God and given to the people. Some will be given the ability to speak in different kinds of tongues, and others will be given the interpretation. As situations arise where the powers of darkness are at work, the ability to distinguish between spirits will be given to particular people. There will constantly be situations that will only find solutions through gifts of faith, healing and miracles.

How does all this happen? First, as leader you must be totally committed to life in the Spirit. That will mean stepping out into uncharted territory. You cannot have every service safely planned if you are going to give room for God to work. He has a habit of upsetting man's best-laid plans!

I believe it is important for Spirit-filled people to have freedom in speaking in tongues. You do not *have* to speak in tongues, but the gift of a prayer language is available to all Spirit-filled believers. As the leader it is important that you speak in tongues and if you have not yet received this gift you can reach out now and God will graciously meet with you.

My brother-in-law Philip (married to Carolyn mentioned at the beginning of this chapter) was so keen to receive the gift that he went out into a park near his home and said to the Lord: 'I'm not leaving here until you give me the gift of tongues.' I am glad to say he was home in time for tea, rejoicing in God's faithfulness.

Paul said: 'I would like every one of you to speak in tongues' (1 Cor 14:5) and later in the chapter: 'I will pray with my spirit, but I will also pray with my mind; I will sing with my spirit, but I will also sing with my mind' (1 Cor 14:15). As you lead people in prophetic gifts and into Spirit-led worship it is essential to be fully liberated yourself in the things of the Spirit.

Let it be clearly understood that spiritual gifts are not the possession of an individual, but are given so that they can pass through you to someone else. The gift of tongues enables God to lead you to pray and use you as the channel for that prayer. When that gift is used for a public utterance, God is speaking a message to his people through you. When tongues is used in singing praise and worship, God is liberating your voice to glorify him and giving you the words and music with which to do it. When a prophecy or other spoken gift is brought, God is using you as a mouthpiece for his word to the people. When faith, healing or miracles are given, here again God uses a human instrument to show his grace to his children.

The gifts of the Holy Spirit often strike me as being like the contents of a tool box. I remember as a child the fascination I experienced every time a carpenter came to our home—I could hardly wait to see the old hessian bag laid open on the floor. There was always the right tool for the job somewhere in that bag. God has given a bag of tools to each of his children so that, whatever the situation, God has the supernatural answer ready and sharpened for use. The Bible says: 'For you can all prophesy in turn so that everyone may be instructed and encouraged' (1 Cor 14:31).

I want to encourage you to step out in faith and expect God to release his gifts through you. God's gifts are for giving. He is always far more ready to give than we are to receive.

There is great joy to be found in seeing people released into using the gifts of the Holy Spirit. Sometimes on a Leaders' Week I will ask for an indication of those who have never received or given a spoken gift of the Holy Spirit. As the show of hands makes known those particular people, I encourage them to look to God expectantly as we worship him, and assure them that God wants to speak through them. And he does.

Before I finish this short section on the gifts of the Holy Spirit, I want to mention the prophetic use of Scripture. A word of prophecy will always be in harmony with Scripture, —often it is straight from the Bible. God will lead someone to read a portion of Scripture, sometimes by giving them the reference of a completely unknown passage, or at other times a familiar part is brought to mind. Listen carefully to the scripture because it is God's particular word for that moment.

The Holy Spirit gives us sensitivity to the voice of God

The indwelling presence of the Holy Spirit enables you to hear the voice of God. In his letter to the Corinthians, Paul carefully explains the difference between the natural man and the spiritual man. (Read 1 Corinthians 2:9–16 in the Authorized Version.) The natural man is not an unconverted man, but a believer who lives by human wisdom and is not sensitive to the voice of God.

Verses 9 and 10 say: 'Eye hath not seen, nor ear heard, neither have entered into the heart of man, the things which God hath prepared for them that love him.' Very often people stop at this point and speak of the ways of God as being unintelligible to mere mortals, but the sentence has not yet ended. It continues: 'But God hath revealed them unto us by his Spirit.'

Paul's argument is this: the man of the Spirit will hear the voice of God, will be taught in the ways of God and will make judgements not according to human reason but by the wisdom that comes from God; but the man who rejects the work of the Spirit will live within the limitations of his own intellect and will consider the things of the Holy Spirit to be unnecessary.

Living in daily dependence on the Holy Spirit is a basic and vital principle if we are to hear God in the way I have explained in Chapter 7.

The Holy Spirit gives anointing

'Anointing' in Scripture has its roots in the Old Covenant where the priests and kings were anointed with oil as they took up office.

The mark of God's anointing is similarly upon lives and ministries today. It has three characteristics: first, it indicates the *confirmation of God* upon a life and role in ministry. An anointed life is one that is totally submitted to the authority of God, and anointed ministry flows out of that relationship with God and the specific call he gives.

You need to operate within the call that has come from God. For example, if God has called you to be an evangelist and you try to become a teacher, you will not enjoy God's anointing upon your teaching, for God will not anoint something that he has not initiated. That does not mean that roles and ministries cannot change; they do, but only under God's direction.

Secondly, anointing is a mark of the *authority of God*. As you fulfil your calling and divine appointment you need to seek God's specific anointing on each aspect of that work. When the anointing comes upon you, you will be conscious of a level of authority that can only come from God. Both you and others will know that such authority does not stem from human capability.

Thirdly, anointing reveals the *character of God*. As you are obedient to your call and live in total dependence upon him, he will be glorified and his character will be revealed. Human sweat, fuss and striving will be absent and the sense of God's peace and blessing will be very evident. This is essential for all who preach and minister, but is equally necessary for those who fulfil more basic roles.

At The Hyde, I encourage those who serve tea and coffee

to seek God's anointing on that task and as they do there comes a sense of the presence of God upon the coffee break that is not of human origin. True anointing always gives the glory to God, not to man.

The Holy Spirit gives power for service

'But you will receive power when the Holy Spirit comes on you' (Acts 1:8). We have seen that Jesus would not let the disciples commence their work without the indwelling power of the Holy Spirit.

Jesus himself did not embark upon his ministry in his power as Son of God, but in the power of the Spirit that came upon him at his baptism. 'And as he was praying, heaven was opened and the Holy Spirit descended on him in bodily form like a dove' (Lk 3:21–22). Following his baptism Jesus was led into the wilderness where he defeated all the onslaughts of Satan in the power of the Spirit. The gospel record goes on to say: 'Jesus returned to Galilee in the power of the Spirit' (Lk 4:14).

If Jesus totally relied upon the Holy Spirit for power, and the apostles were warned not to start upon their work without receiving the Holy Spirit, we are not likely to be able to operate any differently.

However, there is a real danger that we can fall into the trap that caught the Galatians. 'Are you so foolish? After beginning with the Spirit, are you now trying to attain your goal by human effort?' (Gal 3:3).

Each leader who has been called by God will have a God-appointed work assigned to him. You certainly need to know that your work is God-given and not born out of human expectation. Jesus himself did only what his Father told him to do (Jn 5:19–20).

Every part of your life needs to be lived under the anointing of the Holy Spirit or otherwise it will be lived in human strength. If you cannot seek the anointing of God upon some area of your work, you probably should not be doing it. If, despite your prayers, you fail to find any anointing on certain aspects of your work, you need to ask God whether they were part of his plan for you at all or whether they were your own ideas or something imposed upon you by the expectation of others.

Leaders often rob themselves of power because they are not following the pathway of their anointing, but instead are fulfilling all sorts of tasks that 'go with the job'. I will always be thankful for the day when my fellow elder Bob Gordon said to me: 'Charles, I am not going to let you take on responsibilities that will prevent you devoting yourself to the thing that God is really anointing in your life. If you take on things you shouldn't be doing you will lose the anointing on the things you are now doing!'

It is so important to stop doing those things you ought not to be doing, so you can totally give yourself to what you ought to be doing.

The Holy Spirit leads to true praise and worship of God

Jesus said: 'Yet a time is coming and has now come when the true worshippers will worship the Father in spirit and truth, for they are the kind of worshippers the Father seeks. God is spirit, and his worshippers must worship in spirit and in truth' (Jn 4:23–24).

Worship is not the name of a service or a title given to a certain kind of singing, but is the attitude of our lives towards God. In Romans 12:1 we read: 'Therefore, I urge you, brothers, in view of God's mercy, to offer your bodies as living sacrifices, holy and pleasing to God—which is your spiritual worship.' As we acknowledge the greatness of God and his abundant mercy and grace, our lives will be lived to worship him.

Such a life of worship will give rise to times of heartfelt expression of love and praise. As more and more people have entered into the fullness of the Holy Spirit, new songs of praise have emerged. Every move of the Holy Spirit down through the centuries has been accompanied by fresh expressions of praise. It is vital to understand why praise and worship has such a high priority.

God requires our praise and worship. When we are filled with the Holy Spirit, we are filled with the presence of God. The first evidence of his presence will be a desire to praise him. God's work in us always brings glory to him first before anything else. David says: 'I will extol the Lord at all times; his praise will always be on my lips' (Ps 34:1). In Psalm 96:8 we read: 'Ascribe to the Lord the glory due to his name; bring an offering and come into his courts.' Where God is, there will be praise. Heaven is full of worship to God—we catch a glimpse of this in Revelation 4:8: 'Day and night they never stop saying: Holy, holy, holy is the Lord God Almighty, who was, and is, and is to come.'

It is not only a joy, but an act of obedience. There are times when we feel like worshipping, and there are times when we do not. That is why the writer to the Hebrews says: 'Through Jesus, therefore, let us continually offer to God a sacrifice of praise—the fruit of lips that confess his name' (Heb 13:15). A sacrifice is something that is costly. There are many occasions when I do not feel like praising the Lord, but I have learned that as I give of myself in praise to him, my attitude is soon transformed.

I believe Psalm 103 indicates that David may well not have felt like praising God as he climbed out of bed that morning. So he begins by speaking to himself—not the first sign of madness, but the first step towards the presence of God! 'Soul,' he says, 'praise the Lord.' He begins with an act of obedience that is so often the beginning of our praise. He continues: 'Soul, do not forget all the benefits of belonging to God. He forgives all my sins and heals all my diseases; he redeems my life from the pit and crowns me with love and compassion.'

As David continues to declare the faithfulness and greatness of God his spirit rises so much that by the end of the psalm he is shouting to the angels and telling them to join in: 'Praise the Lord, you his angels…. Praise the Lord, all his heavenly hosts!' The devil will always try to stop God's people from worshipping him, because true praise is powerful.

Praise and worship remove self-awareness and give God-awareness. Corporate worship needs to have direction. Coming together to worship is like going on a journey in an aeroplane. We start in the air terminal where there is nothing but noise and bustle. That is similar to all that precedes our going to worship. Sometimes I find our kitchen on a Sunday morning rather like Terminal 3 at Heathrow! From the check-in at the airport we move into the transit lounge where there is less bustle and we know that we are on our way. We settle ourselves ready to worship.

Soon we are seated in the plane and at the end of the runway ready for take-off. There is a great sense of purpose and anticipation, similar to preparing ourselves to come into the presence of God. Take-off is smooth and progressive: likewise, our praise needs to move purposefully heavenward. We begin with songs of joy and songs that declare the greatness and majesty of God.

Those who lead the worship need to know where they are going and the worshippers need to be encouraged to keep their eyes on God. There is nothing worse than what is sometimes called 'sea-sick praise'—with each song spirits rise and hearts are drawn towards God, but as the song ends everyone comes down with a bump as needless talk or other distractions fill the space between one song and the next.

Hymns or songs of praise need to lead onwards and upwards, any spaces being filled with silent worship or prayer so there is an unbroken flow. The worship leaders need to be ready to bring readings from Scripture and to be sensitive to what is happening.

Now the plane has left the runway, operating at full power, and we are rising up through the clouds. Similarly, we pass through the courts of praise and go on into the place of worship. The songs of rejoicing change to songs that are directed to God himself. Now we are not singing *about* God, we are singing *to* him. The majesty of God comes upon us and we are aware of his holy presence, just like breaking through the clouds to the place above where the sun is shining. It has been shining all the time—only we did not see it until we broke through.

The plane levels out and the seat-belt notices are turned off. A tremendous sense of peace descends, as it does in our worship. The singing of songs in our own language may well have given way to singing in God's heavenly language. We know that God is truly among us and we wait in joyful anticipation to hear him speak. We are truly 'lost in wonder, love and praise'.

True worship increases our sensitivity to God's voice and releases his gifts. As we reach the pinnacle of worship we know we are in the presence of God. Therefore, if our worship immediately precedes the preaching there will be a greater receptivity to the word that is given.

The gifts of the Holy Spirit will flow freely when the awesome holy presence of God is among us. There are likely to be words of prophecy, visions, gifts of speaking with tongues and interpretation, the prophetic use of Scripture and words of knowledge and wisdom. If space is allowed for God to move, if we come with expectancy in our hearts and are willing to be used, he will speak.

The healing power of God is particularly present when his people are truly worshipping him. I have known situations where people received healing without anyone praying for them, merely because they were so taken up with the greatness of God that he was able to bypass the self-concern that so often prevents healing, and do his work while they were completely occupied with him!

The lost are won to Christ among the worshipping people of God. 'But if an unbeliever or someone who does not understand comes in while everybody is prophesying, he will be convinced by all that he is a sinner and will be judged by all, and the secrets of his heart will be laid bare. So he will fall down and worship God, exclaiming, "God is really among you!"' (1 Cor 14:24–25).

So much of our evangelism is at an intellectual level where the word is spoken to the mind and received at that level. That is not to say that people do not come to living faith through the intellect, but there are times when the only thing that will really break through into the life of an unbeliever is the majestic presence of the holy God.

Leading people into the realm of the Holy Spirit

1. The baptism with the Holy Spirit

The first step to life in the Holy Spirit is to know that you are filled with the Spirit. I have already explained the clear command in Ephesians: 'Be filled with the Spirit.' It therefore only remains to be obedient to that command. You will not be filled with the Holy Spirit if you are already filled with other things, so it is the pathway of repentance that leads to God's power: repentance from trusting in your own strength, intelligence, training or background; a turning away from self-effort, self-confidence and self-reliance; a coming to God with humility and faith. Paul said: 'I consider everything a loss compared to the surpassing greatness of knowing Christ Jesus my Lord' (Phil 3:8). It is always those who have been believers for many years who find it most difficult to receive the fullness of the Holy Spirit. Spiritual pride and religious tradition are strong barriers to the infilling of the Spirit.

The tremendous promise is that: 'everyone who asks receives' (Lk 11:10) If you are praying for someone to be filled with the Spirit, the following steps need to be taken:

Know the truths of God's word. Turn to the scriptures that speak of God's desire for every one of his children to be filled with the Holy Spirit. A. W. Tozer says:

> Before you are filled with the Holy Spirit you must be sure that you can be filled. The church has tragically neglected this great liberating truth—that there is now for the child of God a full and wonderful and completely satisfying anointing with the Holy Ghost. The Spirit-filled life is not a special, de-luxe edition of Christianity. It is part and parcel of the total plan of God for his people (*The Best of Tozer*, Kingsway Publications 1983, p.207).

Repentance. A person who has been a Christian for some time without being filled with the Spirit will have been relying on human strength and not on God's power, and this will need to be brought to God in repentance.

Lead the person in a prayer of repentance that covers areas of self-effort and pride. Wrong teaching will often have to be laid aside. As he empties himself before the cross of Jesus,

God will fill him with all his love and power.

Be filled now. Ask him simply to invite the Holy Spirit to come more fully into his life. After he has prayed, lay your hands on his head and thank God that he is answering his prayer and, according to the promise of the word, is filling him now.

Do not look for feelings in the person for whom you are praying. He is filled whether he feels anything or not, because God is always faithful to his word.

Thanksgiving and spiritual gifts. Now encourage him to thank God for filling him and to expect to receive spiritual gifts, especially the prayer language of speaking in tongues. Sometimes the person will praise God with other tongues immediately, sometimes it will come later. As in my own case, it may need further prayer and encouragement on another occasion.

The use of other spiritual gifts will come more often in the context of worship and ministry.

2. Praise and worship

We have seen how the Holy Spirit liberates his people to worship him. How then do you lead people into such liberty?

To begin with, a leader needs to be a worshipper himself. It is a worshipping heart that will lead others to worship God, and this is also vital for any musicians involved in leading worship. Although it is important for a musician to be competent with his instrument, musical expertise alone does not release people into worship. You will take people no further in worship than you have come yourself.

It is therefore important that those involved in leading worship not only prepare their music diligently towards excellence, but also prepare their hearts through prayer and praise before attempting to lead others.

It is not my purpose to go into greater detail, but just to say that the dryness of the worship in many churches and groups stems largely from the spiritual state of those who have been given the leadership responsibility.

3. The gifts of the Holy Spirit

God wants his gifts to be used among his people. But how do

you start?

Leaders lead by example. Do what Paul tells you to do: 'eagerly desire spiritual gifts, especially the gift of prophecy' (1 Cor 14:1). As God brings his words through you, the people will follow.

What sometimes happens when a body of people first come into the full blessing of the Spirit is that someone other than the leader manifests a spiritual gift that tends to dominate the whole body. There are situations where things seem to become disorderly and the cry goes out that spiritual gifts must stop. Abuse is not put right by non-use, but by correct use. However, it is the responsibility of leadership to teach the people how to receive and exercise the gifts of the Holy Spirit in a correct manner. 'For God is not a God of disorder but of peace' (1 Cor 14:33).

Prophecy is not to be received without being tested. In certain situations where only one person ever prophesies, there is an unhealthy sense of awe about each pronouncement. I call it the 'in-the-valley-of-the-blind-the-one-eyed-man-is-king' syndrome! Scripture teaches that: 'Two or three prophets should speak, and the others should weigh carefully what is said' (1 Cor 14:29).

Those in leadership have the responsibility to weigh that which is given to the body. In prophecy, there is always content that is entirely from God but at the same time there is often that which may have come from man. That does not mean it all needs to be rejected, but it does need to be weighed. 'For we know in part and we prophesy in part' (1 Cor 13:9).

I do not want to stress the negative side of controlling the gifts, but rather the positive side of encouraging them. If there are only a few among you who have exercised gifts, encourage others to expect God to use them as instruments too. I sometimes tell every person who has ever used one of the gifts to remain quiet, and all those who have never done so to expect God to use them. And as we give time to God in worship he invariably answers that prayer.

12

A Man of the Word

David was exhausted. He had been in such great demand during recent months that his strength was at a very low ebb. This had led to a chest infection that refused to clear up. David, a member of my household, is a fine pianist and leader of praise and worship but had been thoroughly overworked in the Fellowship. If he was not leading worship on Sunday, he would be on a ministry week with me at The Hyde and then, without a break, off travelling with Colin or Bob. And in the gaps there was always someone making demands on him.

There was no doubt he needed a complete break. Fortunately, I have a sister who lives in the Caribbean, and so arrangements were made for him to spend two weeks in St Lucia. As we waved him off, I was glad he was going to rest and have some tropical sunshine, but I wanted to know why he had been overtaken by exhaustion.

There was my own sin for allowing him to take on too much, when I should have made sure that his programme was not so hectic. I had asked David for forgiveness and received it, but I knew there was another reason.

As I was praying about it, I felt the Lord saying to me: 'The problem is that David is living reactively and not creatively.'

I began to understand; David was always so ready to please others that he lived responsively to all the situations that came to him. But God wanted him to live in his creative direction rather than in human reaction.

When David returned, we were able to talk through the whole episode and I discovered that he himself had heard the same word from the Lord during his holiday. We then reordered his programme of work and have now reached a much healthier state of affairs.

God wants us to live as Jesus did, not at the mercy of life's circumstances, but knowing the power of his creative word to transform situations.

The great value of listening to God first thing each morning, (see Chapter 7) is that his is the first voice we hear.

God's word is creative. 'In the beginning God created' are the first five words of the Bible. 'And God said, "Let there be light," and there was light' (Gen 1:3). As God spoke it happened.

A man of the word will make the Scriptures the keystone of his life. 'Remember your leaders, who spoke the word of God to you' (Heb 13:7). Allow the word to have a deep impact on your life, let it work within you so that you become creative in word and deed. Jesus said: 'The words I have spoken to you are spirit and they are life' (Jn 6:63).

The word of God in your life

The Bible is God's revealed word to his people and needs to be received in faith and obedience. It is not my purpose to make a defence of its authenticity, but I say 'Amen' to the reply that was once given concerning its verification: 'Defend the Word of God? I would rather defend a lion. What I say to you is—open the cage and let the word act on its own behalf!'

The evidence for the Scriptures, as far as I am concerned, is the effect they have had on my own life.

God's word convicts. 'The word of God is living and active. Sharper than any double-edged sword, it penetrates even to dividing soul and spirit, joints and marrow; it judges the thoughts and attitudes of the heart' (Heb 4:12). The word reveals the sin in your life as you come to understand God's standard of righteousness. It also uncovers wrong attitudes if you approach it with a willingness for God to deal with you.

In James 1:23–24 it says: 'Anyone who listens to the word but does not do what it says is like a man who looks at his face in a mirror and, after looking at himself, goes away and immediately forgets what he looks like.' Daily reading of the Scriptures can be a painful exercise as God speaks correctively into your life. However, he does not speak to crush or to condemn, but so that you may enter more fully into his freedom and joy. 'It is for freedom that Christ has set us free' (Gal 5:1). The word brings conviction that leads to confession and cleansing.

God's word purifies. The Scriptures also have a purifying effect that is not related to specific sin. Jesus said: 'You are already clean because of the word I have spoken to you' (Jn 15:3) and Paul speaks of 'the washing with water through the word' (Eph 5:26).

This is why in an earlier chapter I recommended reading big chunks of the Bible and allowing the word to soak into you. When I do this I always experience a cleansing and refreshment that is not relative to particular sin, but I know that I have been touched by the purity of a holy God.

God's word gives resistance against temptation. 'I have hidden your word in my heart that I might not sin against you' (Ps 119:11). As you live in the truths of the word, your life is brought into line with God's standards of holiness.

I lived my childhood days under the impact of the words: 'Nothing in all creation is hidden from God's sight' (Heb 4:13). My father would caution me: 'It does not matter whether I can see what you are doing or not, because you cannot hide from God.'

Solomon writes in Proverbs: 'My son, if you accept my words and store up my commands within you...you will understand what is right and just.... Wisdom will save you from the ways of wicked men.... It will save you also from the adulteress, from the wayward wife with her seductive words' (Prov 2:1, 9, 12, 16). I recommend a careful reading of the whole of Proverbs 2.

Leaders are under constant pressure from the circumstances around them. God's word, hidden in your heart, will build your resistance against sin.

I will always remember what Ron Davies, a friend from Zimbabwe, said to me: 'I am not any good at Bible memorization, but when I have hidden a part of God's word in my heart I cannot forget it.'

God's word builds strength. One of the ministers on a recent Leaders' Week gave me this quote: 'Bibles that are falling apart belong to people who are not!' Do not confine the use of your Bible to sermon preparation or you will be in danger of becoming spiritually weak. When using the Scriptures in that way you are receiving a word for others. The word needs to be read for its own sake, to build strength within you.

The psalmist sums it up eloquently in Psalm 19:7 and 8:

> The law of the Lord is perfect,
>   reviving the soul.
> The statutes of the Lord are trustworthy,
>   making wise the simple.
> The precepts of the Lord are right,
>   giving joy to the heart.
> The commands of the Lord are radiant,
>   giving light to the eyes.

God's word gives peace. 'Great peace have they who love your law, and nothing can make them stumble' (Ps 119:165).

You will find a real sense of peace in the life of the person who is saturated in God's word. It is impossible to describe in words, but when you meet that kind of person you know that there is a touch of God's supernatural peace about them.

At a time of great personal turmoil, a song based on the words of Isaiah 26:3 brought God's peace into my heart: 'You will keep in perfect peace him whose mind is steadfast, because he trusts in you.'

The word of God in your thinking

I once heard someone say: 'Ninety-five per cent of my sin is committed in my thought life.'

The sinfulness of man's thinking was exposed by Jesus as he looked beyond the religious exterior of the teachers of the law. 'Knowing their thoughts, Jesus said, "Why do you entertain evil thoughts in your hearts?"' (Mt 9:4). In the Sermon on the Mount we read: '"But I tell you that anyone who looks at a woman lustfully has already committed adultery with her in his heart"' (Mt 5:28). In his letters Paul continues to draw attention to the way society conditions our minds. In Romans 12:2 we read: 'Don't let the world around you squeeze you into its own mould, but let God remould your minds from within' (PHILLIPS).

We need the creative power of God to work upon our minds so that we are not thinking in a natural way but instead in God's way.

This will happen as we live in the word of God daily and receive its truth and light. As the psalmist says: 'How can a young man keep his way pure? By living according to your word' (Ps 119:9). The word provides a creative way of receiving the right stimulus into our minds.

What happens when we are already struggling with negative or impure thoughts? Paul has the answer for us in 2 Corinthians 10:4–5—'We demolish arguments and every pretension that sets itself up against the knowledge of God, and we take captive every thought to make it obedient to Christ.' God gives us the authority over our thought life.

Another important method we can use to develop spiritual thinking is the gift of speaking in tongues. In 1 Corinthians 14:4 we read: 'He who speaks in a tongue edifies himself.' When we pray in tongues we find that God is building up our minds and enabling us to think spiritually. I heard recently of a man who had a ninety-minute car journey to and from work and decided that he would use that time to pray in tongues. His concentration was on his driving, so he released his spirit to be used by God. The result was a mind that was becoming increasingly sensitive to God and less open to erosion by the world.

The word of God in your speech

'The tongue also is a fire, a world of evil among the parts of the body. It corrupts the whole person, sets the whole course of his life on fire, and is itself set on fire by hell' (Jas 3:6). The words we speak have a powerful impact on ourselves and others.

Today's society is full of negative speech: 'What an awful

day!' 'I do feel ill' 'I never get it right' 'I cannot forgive her for what she did to me'. We can so easily become prisoners of the words that fall out of our mouths. As we react to these words in others we become burdened with the heaviness they bring.

God's word is creative: 'Jesus said: "If you hold to my teaching, you are really my disciples. Then you will know the truth, and the truth will set you free"' (Jn 8:31–32). What is the truth that sets you free? It is not facts or circumstances, but the word of God.

Therefore, if your words are born out of the truth of what God has made you in Jesus, and are based on the promises of his word, they will be creative and victorious over negativity.

In James 3:2 we read: 'If anyone is never at fault in what he says, he is a perfect man, able to keep his whole body in check.' In the Bethany Fellowship we call this 'confessing the word'. Colin Urquhart's book *In Christ Jesus* (Hodder & Stoughton, 1981) gives this teaching in great detail and I strongly recommend it to you.

The principle is simply this—everything God says in his word about those who belong to him is true. If we believe it and live by it we will enjoy its benefits. It is most important that our words are in harmony with God's word. Whenever you find the words 'in Christ Jesus', 'through Christ', 'in Christ' or similar in the Scriptures, it is like reading the words of a will that outlines the wealth that has been left for the beneficiaries. Every child of God is a beneficiary of the will Jesus brought into force when he died and rose again. As Paul says to the Corinthians: 'For no matter how many promises God has made, they are "Yes" in Christ. And so through him the "Amen" is spoken by us to the glory of God' (2 Cor 1:20).

When you feel overwhelmed by defeat, you can declare: 'But thanks be to God, who always leads us in triumphal procession in Christ and through us spreads everywhere the fragrance of the knowledge of him' (2 Cor 2:14).

When you feel quite unable to do the task that confronts you, you can say: 'I can do everything through him who gives me strength' (Phil 4:13).

When you are tempted to worry and become anxious,

God's word says: 'Cast all your anxiety on him because he cares for you' (1 Pet 5:7).

When your resources are running out and you do not know how to cope, you can boldly say: 'And my God will meet all your needs according to his glorious riches in Christ Jesus' (Phil 4:19).

This is not mind over matter, but God's creative word which transforms negative words and thoughts that drag you down. As Moses gave God's words to the Israelites he said, 'They are not just idle words for you—they are your life' (Deut 32:47).

The change God wants to make in your speaking requires diligence and application. Look up in a concordance every scripture that tells you who you are 'in Christ', allow these scriptures to become part of you, then ask God to help you change the whole pattern of your speaking. 'For it is with your heart that you believe and are justified, and it is with your mouth that you confess and are saved' (Rom 10:10).

The word of God in your preaching and testimony

Paul encourages Timothy: 'Preach the word' (2 Tim 4:2). Is God's word at the heart of your preaching? What do your people remember when you have finished speaking? Have they received the word of God, or have your own ideas dominated the sermon?

If human thought is the most prominent feature of your preaching, the effect will last only until another more convincing argument is presented to your people. If it is God's word that enters people's lives, his power will change their lives irrevocably. Paul probably had the finest intellect of any preacher living or dead, and yet he said: 'My message and my preaching were not with wise and persuasive words, but with a demonstration of the Spirit's power, so that your faith might not rest on men's wisdom, but on God's power' (1 Cor 2:4–5).

Paul also said: 'Let the word of Christ dwell in you richly as you teach and admonish one another with all wisdom' (Col 3:16). As your life is soaked in the word, your preaching will gain authority and strength.

In 2 Timothy 2:15 we read: 'Do your best to present yourself to God as one approved, a workman who does not need to be ashamed and who correctly handles the word of truth.' I am so thankful now for the many years that were spent in fairly uninspiring Bible Reading meetings in the church where I was brought up. At the time I wondered what was the value of laboriously working through the Scriptures verse by verse. I now realize that I was being taught to be 'a workman who does not need to be ashamed'.

I am afraid there are no short cuts to becoming a craftsman of the word!

There is a particular incident I shall not forget. My mother had gone to the village shop and while she was there a discussion began on a religious topic. As usual, everyone was freely airing their own opinions, when my mother chipped in and began to quote a verse from the Bible. She began by saying: 'Well, Jesus said this…' and went on to quote the appropriate part of Scripture.

The effect was electric—the chatter stopped, everyone listened, and when my mother had finished there was nothing more to be said. Later the story was recounted over the tea table and she added as a postscript: 'It doesn't matter whether they believe the word or not. It is still quick and powerful.'

There are times when we are tempted to speak about what the Bible says instead of simply letting the word speak for itself. You don't need to believe in a sword to get cut by it.

The word of God in personal ministry

'So then faith cometh by hearing, and hearing by the word of God' (Rom 10:17 AV). The more modern versions translate 'word' into 'preaching' or 'message' which is not very accurate. For the Greek word in the original text is *rhema* which carries the sense of a specific word which brings transforming light to the situation.

When involved in personal ministry where a breakthrough is needed, I have often found that a verse of Scripture will come to mind which, when spoken out, completely changes the position.

In personal ministry, you are not only listening to the details being shared by the person, you are also listening to God. You may not find this too easy to begin with; it is something that needs to be cultivated. The *rhema* word you hear may not always be a verse of Scripture, but as it comes from God it will have a creative and dynamic effect. It could come in the form of a word of knowledge or wisdom (1 Cor 12:8) or it might be in the form of a question.

The psalmist says: 'The entrance of your words gives light' (Ps 119:130). It is only as we develop a grasp of God's word that he can bring to our memory those verses that apply to the need of the moment. As God's purpose is to bring wholeness to his people, you will sometimes find that when praying about a physical need, God gives a scripture that goes beyond that to a deeper spiritual need which may have been preventing the desired healing. 'My son, pay attention to what I say; listen closely to my words. Do not let them out of your sight, keep them within your heart; for they are life to those who find them and health to a man's whole body' (Prov 4:20–22).

When I come to the end of a time of personal counselling, I always expect to be guided to the right scriptures to leave with the person as a confirmation of what God has done or as words of faith that will give strength in the days ahead. God is faithful and he invariably brings to mind the right part of his word that seals his work in that person's life. These scriptures may well be in addition to a word of prophecy or a picture that has already been given.

The word of God for direction and guidance

'Your word is a lamp to my feet and a light for my path' (Ps 119:105). Each day we need God's direction for our lives. That is why we must cultivate a daily habit of listening to God. Guidance will not only be heard from that inner voice of God's Spirit, but will also be confirmed by his word.

You will not be likely to hear God by the 'close your eyes

and stick in a pin' method. You may have heard of the man who did this, and on his first attempt fell upon the words: 'Judas went out and hanged himself', which did not encourage him too much. He tried again, and found himself reading these words: 'Go and do likewise'!

I have found that God normally uses those parts of the Bible that are in the flow of my daily reading to bring his specific word of guidance. At other times particular scriptures are brought to mind, and I may well have to use a concordance to discover where they are.

An acute sensitivity needs to be developed for hearing God's voice by his word and by his Spirit so that it becomes a way of life. To come to the Scriptures in a state of panic because you require specific direction or guidance is no way to discover the Lord's will. You need to know that day-by-day confirmation from God that you are walking in his ways. You also need to know that when you go off course you will hear his corrective words. 'Whether you turn to the right or to the left, your ears will hear a voice behind you, saying, "This is the way, walk in it"' (Is 30:21).

How do you live daily in the word? First, make sure you are receiving a regular intake. I mentioned three ways of reading the Bible in Chapter 7.

1. Read one or more chapters at a stretch and allow the message to shower upon you like rain.

2. Then read more slowly, perhaps marking the text in a way that aids concentration and provides useful emphasis later.

3. Learn to meditate on a single phrase or verse.

You may also take a theme that can be followed by using a concordance to find each incidence in Scripture. Bible reading aids are valuable, but can be a mixed blessing. If notes or commentaries are used all the time you can become more influenced by the writer of the notes than by the scriptures themselves. You may refer to various books in study and sermon preparation, but make sure that a good portion of your reading of Scripture is simply in order to allow God to release his meaning and understanding into your heart. A helpful book on the subject is *The Practice of Biblical Meditation* (by Campbell McAlpine, published by Marshall, Morgan &

Scott, 1981).

Well you know that there are times when I get hungry,
So I read your living word, the bread of life.
And Lord you say, 'Delight yourself in fatness,'
So when I dine with you I'm always satisfied.

> O Lord I love your word,
> O Lord I love your word,
> It is life, it is health,
> It is food for my soul,
> O Lord I love your word.
>> (Bryn Haworth from the *Wings of the Morning* album)

13

A Man of Prayer

The Cornwall Mission of 1978 had reached its climax with ten days in Truro Cathedral when a team from St Michael-le-Belfrey, York, had led the worship and David Watson had proclaimed the Christian message each night with clarity and directness.

Having left the family business, I became co-ordinator of the Cornwall Mission and this had filled my time for the previous eighteen months.

Some weeks had passed since the final Mission celebrations in Truro, and I was looking for the next step for me, something new and challenging. For years I had cherished the thought that God might open up the way for a centre in Cornwall which would encourage Christians and build faith. There were a number of options open, and I needed someone to talk to and pray with about them.

I decided to phone John Harper, a friend who was the minister of an Anglican church in St Ives. I knew him to be a man whom I could trust to speak openly and to test what I was hearing from God. A time was fixed, and Joyce and I set off expectantly.

We chatted generally, had some lunch together, and I shared my vision. John listened carefully until I had finished, occasionally asking a question to bring some clarity to a particular point. He did not respond in any specific way, so I nailed him down: 'John, what are you hearing from God?' John's reply was in the form of a question. He said: 'Are you spending time with the Lord daily in quietness and prayer?'

I answered: 'No.'

'Well,' said John, 'that is all I have heard from God. I

suggest that you order your life so as to get your time alone with God each day and then you will be able to hear his direction for your future.'

I went home a little chastened, but knowing that John was right. I had expected to be able to have plenty of time for prayer and Bible study when I entered full-time Christian work, but had discovered that once breakfast was over the demands of my diary and the phone controlled the day.

I had travelled to St Ives with ideas that might have required enough faith to trust God for thousands of pounds. I returned needing faith for the money to buy an alarm clock! For years I had tried to convince God that I could have a satisfactory prayer life without getting out of bed too early. I lost the argument. The psalms often mention early rising: 'I rise before dawn and cry for help' (Ps 119:147).

And so this new way of life began. It was early in the year, and when the alarm rang I would get up and go downstairs to my study, turn the gas fire to a rather quaint setting which said 'miser rate', and meet with God. I cannot say that those times were always full of joy and revelation, because they were not. Many times my rising was in simple obedience to the word I had received from the Lord.

As I stuck at it, my quiet times in the word and prayer became more meaningful and I began to look forward to the early morning. John was right about the future direction of my life. Later on that year God led us to move to Sussex and become part of the Bethany Fellowship.

Personal prayer: a daily priority

That early time has become a priority in my life, and as the years have gone by I have found the need to develop and structure those first few hours of the day.

Each day, before the demands of ministry begin, I need to have prayed with my wife, the other adults who are part of my family and with my children, in addition to a personal time of quiet. This may seem quite a programme, and indeed it is, but I have not found any way to accomplish it satisfactorily without rising early.

The regular time in the morning praying with Joyce came about because I discovered that when many hours of my day might be given to prayer, the one area that was receiving no real prayer cover was my family life. Attempts at praying at night failed because of tiredness. And so I get up early, make a cup of tea and we sit up in bed and spend time in worship and prayer. We are able to pray through any difficulties that the children are experiencing and know too that our hearts are in tune with God and with each other.

It is a normal practice in the Fellowship for all the adults to meet together for prayer early in the morning. The five adults of our household, Joyce, David, Rosie, Lyn and myself, meet for half an hour each morning. As we are all involved in doing different things, we can pray through the details of the day and also spend time corporately listening to God and worshipping him.

We discovered by trial and error that pre-breakfast is the best time for our family prayers. The five children join the adults after our prayer time and we read the Bible together and also some other book which has both interest for the children and spiritual significance. We then all pray at a level that is appropriate to the children. No long prayers and no one not praying!

I also make time each day for listening to God and writing down in a book what I am hearing from him (see Chapter 7) and for personal Bible reading and prayer.

The result of all this is that I am at peace with Joyce and there is peace in our home. The children leave for school with their day covered in prayer and at peace with each other and God. The household can go to their various responsibilities with that same sense of order, and I can get into the day with the assurance that God is in control.

The routine can be adapted if we get to bed very late one night or the alarm fails to ring. The routine does not run us. It is, however, the regular pattern of our lives and has been devised not legalistically but as a means of approaching each day in the awareness of God.

Prayer is a vital necessity

This chapter is not intended to give detailed teaching, but to show how a leader's work needs to be born out of prayer in every area of life and at every point of activity.

There was a time when I was amazed at a statement made by Martin Luther, the gist of which was: the busier the day, the longer he needed to pray before it began. On some occasions this required three hours of prayer. I have not quite managed to emulate the number of hours, but I certainly identify with the principle.

In Chapter 5 I wrote of how the revival weekend transformed the Fellowship's prayer life and how we found we needed about two hours of prayer before each mission meeting. That transformation has continued. During elders' meetings, unhurried time is given to prayer and seeking God. Our leadership groups also give much time to prayer.

For the Leaders' Weeks I work with a team of about twelve people. I see the primary purpose of the team to be a prayer force to undergird the ministry of these Weeks, so we meet regularly for days of prayer and fasting between the Weeks, and during a Week itself we meet for forty-five minutes prior to the morning meeting and for an hour before the evening meeting. Time and again we spend that hour seeking God, because we know that unless he acts nothing will be achieved.

Prayer declares that only God can do it

When a leader allows prayer to be eroded from his life, he is in fact saying: 'God, I do not need you, I can get along quite well on my own.'

When a church council or a gathering of elders and deacons places prayer merely in the formalities that open and close their meetings, they are saying: 'We can make better decisions by our discussion than by hearing the mind of God.'.

When a church does not have prayer gatherings as part of its regular life, the same thing is being said.

In 2 Chronicles 20:12, King Jehoshaphat cries out to God: 'We do not know what to do, but our eyes are upon you.'

What priority do you give to prayer?

Prayer leads to humility

When a man prays, he is acknowledging that God is greater than he is. He is admitting need and may well be acknowledging failure. It is pride that leads to prayerlessness. 'God opposes the proud but gives grace to the humble' (1 Pet 5:5).

The word of the Lord to Solomon was: 'if my people, who are called by my name, will humble themselves and pray and seek my face and turn from their wicked ways, then will I hear from heaven and will forgive their sin and will heal their land' (2 Chron 7:14).

The devil will seek to thwart every attempt that is made to set aside time for prayer because he knows how powerful it is. You may well have heard the couplet:

> The devil trembles when he sees
> The weakest saint upon his knees.

It may be trite, but that doesn't stop it being true.

Prayer brings unity

Prayer that is powerful acknowledges the greatness of God, as did King Jehoshaphat: 'O Lord, God of our fathers, are you not the God who is in heaven? You rule over all the kingdoms of the nations. Power and might are in your hand, and no one can withstand you' (2 Chron 20:6).

It is important that times of corporate prayer are set in the context of praise and worship, because as you declare the greatness of God in your praise, you come into right relationship with God. It is also important that revival principles are operative when praying with others, so that sin is confessed and fellow believers walk in the light together. As we come into God's holy presence and his light shines into our hearts, all darkness is exposed. That will lead to confession and cleansing, because 'if I had cherished sin in my heart, the Lord would not have listened' (Ps 66:18).

It is not only sin against God that shuts his ears to our prayers, but also sin and unforgiveness towards others. Do you know that the statement: 'The prayer of a righteous man is powerful and effective' in James 5:16 is immediately preceded by: 'Therefore confess your sins to each other and pray for each other so that you may be healed'?

Scripture shows that effective group prayer will begin with each person having an assurance through confession to God and to one another that there is no area of darkness.

As you come to pray together, acknowledging these principles, be ready to examine your hearts so that you have that assurance of complete unity with one another. 'How good and pleasant it is when brothers live together in unity!.... For there the Lord bestows his blessing, even life for evermore' (Ps 133:1, 3).

Agreeing prayer: a powerful dynamic

Jesus said: '"Again, I tell you that if two of you on earth agree about anything you ask for, it will be done for you by my Father in heaven"' (Mt 18:19).

Powerful prayer begins when two are in agreement. That is why the prayers of a husband and wife have such power potential. This verse is not saying that if any two people agree on some idea or notion that they are automatically going to receive the answer to their prayer. The agreement that is meant is the agreement of hearts that together can hear the mind of God and so in their unity receive the answer to their prayer.

I remember David Watson telling me how in the early days at St Cuthbert's, when he had taken over an empty church, it was the weekly day of prayer and fasting with his wife Anne that was the key to the success that was to follow.

I value my Leaders' Week team greatly, because I know that in the heart agreement God has given us lies the key to power in prayer.

Whenever I travel to take church weekends or conferences, again I choose a team primarily for their prayer support. It is a principle of the Fellowship that no one goes out on ministry alone, because at least one other person is needed with whom there can be agreement in prayer.

I imagine that is why Paul always had a travelling companion—Barnabas, Silas or Timothy.

Prayer achieves victory

2 Chronicles 20 gives a fine example of how victory is achieved by prayer.

King Jehoshaphat was being attacked by the armies of Moab and Ammon, and all the human indications were that he was in for quite a beating. So what did he do? First, he called all the people to fast and pray (v.3). He then led them in prayer to God. He started by declaring the might and power of God (v.6) and continued by stating his commitment to look to God for the answer (v.9).

He even had a good moan about the circumstances that had led to the crisis (vv.10 and 11), but ended by that unequivocal statement of faith and trust in God: 'We do not know what to do, but our eyes are upon you' (v.12).

As the people stood in prayer before God (v.13), a prophetic word was given to Jahaziel which brought God's answer to the people: 'stand firm and see the deliverance the Lord will give you' (v.17).

Jehoshaphat acted upon the God-given word and sent the choir out at the head of the army. 'Jehoshaphat appointed men to sing to the Lord and to praise him for the splendour of his holiness as they went out at the head of the army' (v.21).

As they went out the Lord gave them a mighty victory and was true to his word to the last detail (vv.22 and 23). The people gratefully gave thanks to God (v.28).

It then says: 'The fear of God came upon all the kingdoms of the countries when they heard how the Lord had fought against the enemies of Israel' (v.29).

In the days that followed the revival weekend at The Hyde that I wrote about in Chapter 5, God taught us how to pray through to victory. The principles are the same as those followed by Jehoshaphat:

1. A commitment to pray and seek God (v.3).
2. The declaration of God's mighty power (v.6).
3. A refusal to look anywhere but to God (v.9).
4. A realistic appraisal of the situation (vv.10 and 11).
5. A statement of faith and trust (v.12).
6. A waiting upon God for his answer (v.13). For this God has given us His Spirit:

> In the same way, the Spirit helps us in our weakness. We do not know what we ought to pray, but the Spirit himself intercedes for us with groans that words cannot express. And he who searches our hearts knows the mind of the Spirit, because the Spirit intercedes for the saints in accordance with God's will (Rom 8:26–27).

7. God's answer was given (v.17).
8. They fell down in worship before the Lord (v.18).
9. God's answer was received and acted upon (v.21).
10. Action followed that fulfilled all that had gone before (vv.22 and 23).
11. They did not forget to give God the glory (v.28).

Victory is achieved by prayer and must be received by a step of faith. A parallel New Testament example is given in Acts 4:23–31.

The gifts of the Spirit in prayer

The word that God gave to Jahaziel in 2 Chronicles 20 may seem all too easy and neat and you might ask—does God speak to us like that today? The answer is 'yes'.

God has given us the gifts of his Holy Spirit so that he can reveal his purpose to us and through us. 'In the same way no-one knows the thoughts of God except the Spirit of God. We have not received the spirit of the world but the Spirit who is from God, that we may understand what God has freely given us (1 Cor 2:11–12).

Therefore, as we meet together to pray through a situation we need to be ready to receive a word from God that will give the answer to our prayer and the assurance of victory. 'Now to each one the manifestation of the Spirit is given for the common good. To one there is given through the Spirit the message of wisdom, to another the message of knowledge by means of the same Spirit…to another prophecy, to another the ability to distinguish between spirits, to another the ability to speak in different kinds of tongues, and to still another the interpretation of tongues' (1 Cor 12:7–10).

After opening up a situation before the Lord, I have often found that the time of waiting for his answer is given to praying in the Spirit: 'We do not know what we ought to pray, but the Spirit himself intercedes for us' (Rom 8:26). When the prophetic word is received it is rather like an interpretation to what may have been a lengthy period of praying in tongues.

The word from the Lord may come in any number of ways. It may be through a passage of Scripture that is given to one person, or it could be a prophetic picture given to another. The spoken gifts of the Holy Spirit of prophecy, wisdom, knowledge, tongues and interpretation are all available to God's people so that God can reveal his mind and purposes.

Do not let your prayers be all one-way. Give time and space for God to give the answer.

Pray without ceasing

The apostle Paul has a habit of writing certain devastating truths, in brief and without comment or explanation, like this: 'Be joyful always; pray continually; give thanks in all circumstances, for this is God's will for you in Christ Jesus' (1 Thess 5:16).

How can we pray continually?

First, if you are constantly aware of the need to see God at work in every situation you will live in an attitude of continuous prayer. There will be a God-centredness about you and you will be focused on God at all times, looking to him for his divine intervention and activity.

God has also made available to his people the gift of praying in other tongues. 1 Corinthians 14:14 says: 'For if I pray in a tongue, my spirit prays, but my mind is unfruitful.'

Therefore, you can pray in tongues at times when your mind is centred on other things. Jackie Pullinger, whose story is told in the book *Chasing the Dragon* (Hodder & Stoughton, 1980) prayed in tongues constantly throughout each day and the result was a tremendous release of God's power in the 'red light' area of Hong Kong.

A car journey is a useful time to pray in the Spirit, also when doing household chores. Praying in the Spirit enlarges one's perception of what God will do. 'He who speaks in a tongue edifies himself' (1 Cor 14:4).

There are times when you may be led to pray in the Spirit for a considerable length of time and only later discover that there was some crisis taking place at that particular time and God was able to use you as an intercessor.

Prayer with fasting

If you are serious about prayer, you will also begin to see the importance of prayer with fasting. 'Blow the trumpet in Zion, declare a holy fast, call a sacred assembly. Gather the people, consecrate the assembly; bring together the elders, gather the children' (Joel 2:15–16).

There will be many times when answers to prayer are not easily received. There is no slick and easy way to receive answers. As prayer becomes the breath of your spiritual life, you will live in the flow of God's answers, but you will also come up against situations that are stubborn and for which no answer seems forthcoming. At these times, prayer with fasting will help. However, it is wrong to believe that whenever there is some difficulty a day of prayer and fasting will be the panacea.

Just as with prayer, fasting needs to become a way of life, and as it becomes a regular feature of your spiritual discipline, you will begin to appreciate its value.

I recommend that you look up every reference in the Bible where fasting is mentioned, write them all down and allow God to speak to you from his word concerning this discipline. There are also a number of helpful books available on the subject.

Prayer produces peace

'Let the peace of Christ rule in your hearts, since as members of one body you were called to peace. And be thankful' (Col 3:15).

Peace is the hallmark of a life lived in dependence on God. Many times it is not praying through to victory that is needed, but praying through to peace. There are times when a situation will break upon you suddenly, robbing you of peace and throwing you into turmoil and confusion. What do you do?

The temptation is to worry and fret and hunt around for a human answer. What is needed is a time of prayer alone or with someone else. There have been many occasions at The Hyde when someone will ask me to join them in praying over a situation that has arisen through a phone call or because of some sudden crisis. We will stand quietly before God and pray through to the place of peace. If I am at home my wife and I, plus any other member of the household who is about, will stop whatever we are doing and bring that need to our loving heavenly Father who has all knowledge and understanding.

When peace has been received, we can respond creatively instead of reactively. We can hear God's answer and step out to act with faith and assurance.

Prayer in personal ministry

'It all happens as you pray,' is one of those phrases that have become part of the jargon of our Fellowship. When involved in ministering to an individual, you need to beware of trying to meet the need or solve the problem merely by good advice. There is no doubt that as you speak, you will be given wisdom from God, but the activity of God's power in that person's life will happen as you pray.

Everything you say and do needs to be preparing a pathway for the time of prayer when God steps in and does the work that no man can imitate.

I have already mentioned situations when you will be

praying for people to receive new life in Christ, and to be filled with the Holy Spirit. Whatever the need is, it is in the place of prayer that God's eternal work is done.

Prayer is communion with God

'One of those days Jesus went out into the hills to pray, and spent the night praying to God' (Lk 6:12). The essence of prayer is communion with the Father. The more you spend time in his holy presence, the more you will want to spend time with him.

You will also begin to understand something of the Father's heart of love towards mankind. You will receive whatever you ask as you learn to pray according to the will of God: 'because the Spirit intercedes for the saints in accordance with God's will' (Rom 8:27).

I spent fifteen years working in the family business. My father was the Managing Director and I was immediately under his authority. Often, members of staff would ask me for decisions on matters relating to their department or area of responsibility. Because I knew fairly accurately what my father's response would be, I could give them a ready reply. As I had taken time to learn how my father thought and acted, I was able to operate confidently in that context.

As you learn to seek God, you will not only get to know him better, but your confidence in him will grow as you see his mighty hand at work.

14

A Man of Faith

We had been meeting as a small home prayer group for a number of months. We often ate supper together before our meetings, and our fellowship was good, but the praise and worship was a bit stilted and the prayer was variable. It was one of those regular steady groups, in which not a great deal ever happened, and where not much was expected to happen either.

That is, until Arthur arrived among us. He had become a Christian about six months earlier in the middle of a marriage breakdown crisis. In the months that followed he had embarked upon nursing training in a nearby hospital. Because of his shift work, he arrived late at the meeting that night and slipped in when the praying had already begun.

He had only been there five minutes when, during a moment's silence, he spoke out: 'Would someone please pray for me? Today I injured my back through lifting one of the patients. I know that if someone prays for me I will be healed.'

Silence again fell. After about thirty seconds, I ventured a look around the room to see which of my faith-filled friends would jump up and pray the prayer of healing. No one stirred.

I thought: 'I can't let poor Arthur just sit there with no one praying for him, and yet I don't feel I have enough faith to believe God would heal him through my prayer.' I tussled with my conflicting emotions. As no one had moved in what seemed an eternity of highly charged silence, I went over to Arthur and tentatively laid my hands on his shoulders. I drew in a deep breath and prayed with as much faith as I could muster.

After I had finished the prayer, I went back to my place and sat down, and the prayer meeting continued in its normal fashion!

When we finished, we had some coffee together and went home. I did not dare ask Arthur whether anything had happened to him. My faith did not stretch that far.

The next evening as we were about to start our meal, Arthur bounced in the door. The words fell from his lips in a torrent: 'You know, when you prayed for me last night I had a burning sensation right through my back and I knew I was healed. Today, I have lifted patients in and out of bed all day and haven't had one twinge of pain. Hallelujah!'

I was full of joy and profound relief. I had not felt a thing as I had prayed for him. God was beginning to teach me something about faith.

Faith: a vital necessity

'Remember your leaders...and imitate their faith' (Heb 13:7). If faith is to be followed, the reality of faith must be seen in the leader's life.

Hebrews 11:6 is a very uncomfortable verse of Scripture. It says: 'And without faith it is impossible to please God'. I would have preferred the verse to have said 'it is difficult'. The word 'impossible' is totally uncompromising and we all need to face up to its implications.

To live in faith is to know that all you are is from God. You are to live God's life in his strength, under his direction, according to his will and purpose and to his glory. To live in natural human strength and ability is not faith and does not please God.

In Paul's doxology in Romans 11:35 and 36 he writes: 'Who has ever given to God, that God should repay him? For from him and through him and to him are all things. To him be the glory for ever! Amen.'

The sobering fact is this: it is only that which God does in your life that has any eternal value, and it is only the power God pours through you that has any effect upon the lives of others.

You need faith to receive God's life and power and you need faith to transmit that life and power to others. That faith is a revelation from God.

Faith: an unfolding revelation

'Now faith is being sure of what we hope for and certain of what we do not see' (Heb 11:1). Faith is more sure of the invisible than the visible. By faith, my life in Christ is more real than my natural life, even though I cannot put it in a test tube and subject it to scientific tests. The reality of God is more tangible to me than the chair in which I am sitting writing these words.

God commended the saints of old because they acted upon his word instead of on human logic. In fact, the whole of Hebrews 11 recounts one incident after another where men of faith obeyed God in the face of all the odds. They were counted foolish in the eyes of the world, but because they saw beyond this life to God's timeless purposes, they obeyed and received his blessing as a result.

Faith is a gift from God that enables us to receive the eternal realities he makes available.

Faith for salvation

'Therefore, since we have been justified through faith, we have peace with God through our Lord Jesus Christ' (Rom 5:1). As the gospel is declared you are faced up to the truth of the sin and disobedience that have separated you from God. You have a choice at that point, whether to disregard what you have heard or to reach out to God and receive his new life through repentance and faith.

Even repentance is a gift from God. Acts 5:31 says: 'God exalted him to his own right hand as Prince and Saviour that he might give repentance and forgiveness of sins to Israel.' When Peter was asked to visit Cornelius and his household he was not sure whether God would accept Gentiles. After the Holy Spirit had been poured out on them so powerfully, Peter was hauled in front of the other apostles to account for his actions. When they heard what had happened they praised God, saying: 'So then, God has even granted the Gentiles repentance unto life' (Acts 11:18).

At the moment of repentance and faith you receive the revelation of the new life in Christ, you are justified by faith and you receive peace with God as the confirmation. You have been made righteous through Christ. The life that is received by faith must continue in faith: 'For in the gospel a righteousness from God is revealed, a righteousness that is by faith from first to last, just as it is written: "The righteous will live by faith"' (Rom 1:17).

Faith for God's power

The revelation is unfolding. You have the life of Christ through faith in him. You are 'a new creation; the old has gone, the new has come!' (2 Cor 5:17). It is like acquiring a brand-new car. The old banger has been pushed away to the breakers' yard, and the new vehicle stands in all its glory. But in order for that car to be enjoyed to the full, you need to put petrol in the tank.

The Holy Spirit is available to every child of God and is received by faith. Paul says in 1 Corinthians 2:4 and 5: 'My message and my preaching were not with wise and persuasive words, but with a demonstration of the Spirit's power, so that your faith might not rest on men's wisdom, but on God's power.'

By faith you live daily in the reality of the Spirit's power.

However, it is possible to begin in the power of the Spirit and then lapse into human effort. This happened to the Galatian Christians. 'Are you so foolish? After beginning with the Spirit, are you now trying to attain your goal by human effort? Have you suffered so much for nothing—if it really was for nothing? Does God give you his Spirit and work miracles among you because you observe the law, or because you believe what you heard?' (Gal 3:3–5).

Faith that brings healing

As the age of the Spirit began, all kinds of things started happening that caused the religious people of the day to ask searching questions.

Peter and John were quietly minding their own business, taking a stroll to the temple to pray, when a cripple confronted them with a common request in those days. Peter and John had a choice: they could rummage around in their pockets and find a small coin to silence the poor beggar, or they could step out in faith. It so happened that they had come away without any money. God has a real sense of humour. He lands his children into impossible situations when the only thing they can do is to look to him for a miracle.

So Peter said: '"Silver or gold I do not have, but what I have I give you. In the name of Jesus Christ of Nazareth, walk." Taking him by the right hand, he helped him up, and instantly the man's feet and ankles became strong. He jumped to his feet and began to walk' (Acts 3:6–7).

This caused quite a stir among the people and they crowded around Peter and John looking for an explanation. Peter's statement is clear: 'By faith in the name of Jesus, this man whom you see and know was made strong. It is Jesus' name and the faith that comes through him that has given this complete healing to him, as you can all see' (Acts 3:16).

Those early disciples were beginning to receive the faith that knows that nothing is impossible with God.

God is always ready to reward a step of faith, and very often when someone is new to the whole realm he will encourage their faith with a mighty miracle, as he did with Peter and John. Therefore, step out in faith.

Faith to live the crucified life

Saul, that arch-persecutor of the new Christian church, had met God on the Damascus Road. His life had been transformed and his name had been changed to Paul.

I do not know what Paul thought was going to be in store for him when he became a believer, but even as Ananias was being sent to pray with him to be filled with the Holy Spirit and receive his sight, the Lord revealed something of the cost of his new calling. 'But the Lord said to Ananias, "Go! This man is my chosen instrument to carry my name before the Gentiles and their kings and before the people of Israel. I will show him how much he must suffer for my name"' (Acts 9:15–16).

God's calling upon your life will involve cost and suffering. That will require faith, because there is no way you can live the life to which God has called you without his supernatural power and resources.

Len Moules was a great challenge and blessing to me when I was a young Christian. It was evident that God had done a very deep work in his life. It was not until I read his biography *On to the Summit* by Pat Wraight (Kingsway/CLC, 1981) that I learned something of the secret. I quote the incident in full because it has a powerful message for all in leadership. Len is speaking:

> One morning the father of one of our missionaries, who was staying with us, asked me if I would go with him for an early walk. I thought he wanted to see the dawn on the Himalayan snows. So I took him to a certain point and said, 'That's the first peak that really gets the sun.' He said, 'I haven't come to see the dawn, I've come to chat with you.'
>
> And I had an anxious feeling down in my stomach that he had something serious to say. He had. We sat down and he asked, 'Len, do you know Galatians 2:20?' Thank God, I did; and I began to recite it: 'I have been crucified with Christ; it is no longer I who live, but Christ who lives in me; and the life I now live in the flesh I live by faith in the Son of God, who loved me and gave himself for me.'
>
> In fact I never completed it, because half-way through he stopped me and said, 'Len, I know you can say it, but what do you know of it? I thank you, Len, for letting me be with you at this conference, to see you plan on the blackboard where you are going to put your missionaries. That was not Spirit planning, that was human efficiency in the use of your missionaries. It wasn't God-given.
>
> 'Len, I've heard you praying. Oh that I could say it was the Spirit at prayer, but it wasn't. It was you praying with all your

human desires, asking God's blessing on it.

'You have fun at the table. If only I could feel it was Christ rejoicing in your midst, but not from you, Len. You are such a human human, Len, you know nothing of this. Oh, I know that you'd be willing to give your body to be burned, but Len, it is just in the energy of the flesh and you're asking God to bless it. You know nothing of this verse of Scripture.'

And he left me.

It wasn't long after, possibly an hour later, that dawn came on the peaks, but that didn't exist as far as I was concerned. I was face to face with God on this issue. Thirteen years as a missionary—and if those works had been tested by fire no doubt they would have gone up as wood, hay and stubble. Human plans, human initiative, human ideas—good ideas. What I thought was best, sacrifice and what not, but was it the Lord's will? Was it spiritual decision? I doubt it. I know it wasn't. An hour later I lay down on the grass on that mountainside and spread my arms wide and said,

'Lord, I am crucified with you. Oh, I live. Thank God for strength and a mind and a heart and a will and emotions and love. Thank you, Lord, I live, but not I, but you live through me.'

Faith is not a static thing, but an unfolding revelation of the power and character of God which needs to be grasped with an ever-increasing intensity.

The reality of faith

You will have realized through what I have already shared of my own faith pilgrimage, that to have received the life, power and healing of Jesus is no guarantee that you will have confidence to minister it to others.

For many years I could not believe that God would work in others if I were to pray for them. To be asked to pray for someone threw me into panic and fear.

It was not that I doubted *God's* ability to meet with all those who came to him in faith: my doubt was that God could actually use *me*.

During Leaders' Weeks, I have often found this same fear and uncertainty in people who have been in a pastoral ministry for many years. This has usually resulted in stagnation in their churches. For even though the truth has been faithfully proclaimed, the failure to bring people through one by one to freedom in Christ has spelt defeat and sometimes despair.

I know of ministers who have a very powerful pulpit ministry but who see very little happening in their people because of a failure to give opportunity for personal ministry that carries through the message that has been preached.

In a pastoral situation two things need to happen. First, you need a level of faith that gives you God-given confidence to exercise an effective personal ministry, and secondly you need to be bold in confronting people with the demands of God.

By the words 'confronting people', I do not mean that you are for ever creating situations of conflict, but that you accept the responsibility of ministering through the work of grace that is necessary for each person.

In James's letter there is some clear teaching about faith and deeds. 'But someone will say, "You have faith; I have deeds." Show me your faith without deeds, and I will show you my faith by what I do' (Jas 2:18).

In the context of this chapter, the deeds of faith are the actions that bring about a supernatural work in your people.

In his definition of faith Jesus says: 'Therefore I tell you, whatever you ask for in prayer, believe that you have received it, and it will be yours' (Mk 11:24). Faith has received the answer before you embark upon personal ministry. If a person is coming to you to commit his life to Christ, receive that new life from God in faith before you enter the room to pray with him. You know that as you lead that person to the cross of Jesus they will receive the life of Christ. There is no doubt about it.

How do you receive this reality of faith? There is a definite progression that leads to growth in faith for ministry.

Faith in Christ, the Son of the living God

Something happened in the life of Peter when he confessed: '"You are the Christ, the Son of the living God"' (Mt 16:16).

Jesus told him that his declaration had not come out of his human understanding but by revelation from God.

In speaking those words Peter was doing more than stating a theological fact, he was declaring a dynamic truth. When you receive the revelation that Jesus Christ is the Son of the living God and that you are a 'son of God', you will know that whatever you ask in the name of Jesus, he will do (Jn 14:13). That is a life changing truth.

Jesus went on in Matthew 16 to speak about the rock on which he would build his church. I do not believe the rock was Peter, but that the confession he made—that Jesus was the Christ, the Son of the living God—was the rock. Immediately Jesus declared that the gates of Hades would not overcome the church that is built on the true Christ in all his powerful authority.

To say that Peter was the rock is to declare that the new church was to be built upon a man. A study of the epistles demonstrates over and over again that the first disciples built their lives and ministries upon the declaration of a living Christ, one who continues to act with power and authority in the lives of men.

He went on to say: "'I will give you the keys of the kingdom of heaven; whatever you bind on earth will be bound in heaven, and whatever you loose on earth will be loosed in heaven'" (Mt 16:19). If you have received God-given understanding of the authority of the kingdom you will exercise a ministry that has the hallmark of that kingdom.

The foundation upon which the church is built is faith in a great God who is able to do great things in the lives of mankind and the measure of your faith is determined by the degree of your heart knowledge of the sovereignty of God.

Mustard seed faith

How then does this growth of faith begin? When the disciples came to Jesus after they had failed to set the epileptic boy free, they said to him: "'Why couldn't we drive it out?" He replied, "Because you have so little faith. I tell you the truth, if you have faith as small as a mustard seed, you can say to this mountain, 'Move from here to there' and it will move. Nothing will be impossible for you"' (Mt 17:19–21).

They required a mustard seed faith. If you are willing to step out boldly in faith, God readily plants that mustard seed within you. It is exciting and demanding. It is exciting because nothing will be impossible for you as you allow God to release his power through you. It will be demanding because the growth of that faith will place you into situations where you will have to trust God in the face of seemingly impossible odds.

That is the challenge. If you are prepared to say to God: 'I am ready for anything', he will lead you out into a thrilling adventure. The reason so few people step out into daring faith is that it is costly. It will demand nothing short of everything. You will give God the opportunity of creating the initiative and your life of peace and quiet will have ended for ever. You will live in the realization that every predicament that confronts you is beyond your natural resources, and you will be crying out to God: 'If you don't do something here Lord, I'm sunk.' Just as things look hopeless, God will step in and you will fall to your knees in praise and gratitude to God for his power and faithfulness.

Faith thresholds: how faith can grow

1. *The measure of faith*

It is no good wishing you were someone else. You have to begin by accepting that God has made you just as you are because he wanted it that way. He does not want you to stay as you are, but he does want you to begin as you are. If you try to copy someone else you will never develop in faith. Unreality, trying to be something you are not, is one of the biggest barriers to spiritual progress. 'Surely you desire truth in the inner parts, you teach me wisdom in the inmost place' (Ps 51:6). I have yet to discover a way to help someone who has an unrealistic opinion of his own faith in ministry.

Paul wrote: 'For by the grace given me I say to every one of you: Do not think of yourself more highly than you ought, but rather think of yourself with sober judgment, in accordance with the measure of faith God has given you' (Rom 12:3).

So begin by thanking God for who you are and for the measure of faith you have been given. Tell him that you want to grow in faith and that you are ready to respond to every situation he puts in front of you.

That is the pathway God has shown me. It is not the situations I have initiated that have provided stimuli to faith, but those where I have been 'dropped in at the deep end', like the one that opens this chapter. If you tell God that you are ready for anything, he will take you at your word!

2. *Increase our faith*

In one of those humorous parts of the Bible that make me chuckle as I try to imagine the scene, Jesus is teaching his disciples about forgiveness. He suggests that if your brother sins against you seven times in one day, and seven times comes back to you and says 'I repent', that you forgive him each time. The disciples' response is: 'Increase our faith!' (Lk 17:3–5).

Notwithstanding the humour of this situation, the truth is that it is possible to see your faith increase. As one called to ministry, it is my constant prayer: 'Lord, increase my faith.' Every time I minister in the name of Jesus I want to see God do new and greater things than ever before. I do not always see the increase, but my prayer remains, and I know God is answering that prayer and the mustard seed of faith is growing into a tree of faith.

3. *The environment of faith*

There is a level of faith among a group of believers that creates the environment in which God can work. As members of the Fellowship travel around, we become aware of the different levels of faith in the various churches and meetings where we minister. Sometimes it is high and expectant, at other times low and depressive. This is in no way intended as a value judgement on anyone, but a fact of which no leader should be ignorant.

Paul said: 'Our hope is that, as your faith continues to grow, our area of activity among you will greatly expand'

(2 Cor 10:15). Paul wanted to see the faith of these believers grow for he knew that as that happened, the work of the gospel would increase. It is of little value for a minister to be praying for an increase of faith for himself if he is not bringing about a corporate increase of faith in the people who have already committed their lives to Christ.

As the Leaders' Week team and I pray together, my faith is strengthened, but I fully accept my responsibility to build faith in them so that together we can know a greater effectiveness in the ministry to which God has called us.

When Jesus went to Nazareth we read that he did not perform many miracles, and the Scriptures explain the reason why: 'And he did not do many miracles there because of their lack of faith' (Mt 13:58).

If Jesus was prevented from seeing victory through his ministry because of a lack of faith in the people, how much more should we concentrate on building the faith and expectancy of our people.

4. Faith built by the word

'"The word is near you; it is in your mouth and in your heart," that is, the word of faith we are proclaiming: That if you confess with your mouth, "Jesus is Lord;" and believe in your heart that God raised him from the dead, you will be saved' (Rom 10:8–9). The passage speaks of the word of faith concerning salvation in Jesus. As they received it in their hearts and spoke it out with their mouths, so their lives were transformed.

The Bible is the record of almighty God who throughout history has intervened in the lives of men in response to faith. As you feed upon the word in your own personal devotions, and as you declare the word from the pulpit, and as you live by the word in every area of your life, faith will grow in your heart and in the hearts of your people.

Do you know where your threshold of faith is today? When did it last move? If your heart is set upon seeking God, you will be constantly aware of the growth of faith within you. That will mean an increasing fruitfulness in your life and ministry that you may once have thought impossible. In addition, God's holy presence will become more real to you and will have its own transforming and purifying effect.

The scope of faith

When do you reach the limit of faith? You do not. Jesus said: 'anyone who has faith in me will do what I have been doing. He will do even greater things than these, because I am going to the Father' (Jn 14:12).

That verse has a most stimulating effect on every man of faith. You know that there is always more of God's power and activity that you have not yet seen. He is always ready to do more in response to faith, so you press on with him.

'This is love for God: to obey his commands. And his commands are not burdensome, for everyone born of God overcomes the world. This is the victory that has overcome the world, even our faith. Who is it that overcomes the world? Only he who believes that Jesus is the Son of God' (1 Jn 5:3–5).

15

A Man of Humility

The problem with humility is that it is a quality we know we ought to possess, yet its presence is more readily seen in us by others than by ourselves. Who would admit to being proud and arrogant?

I find that I live with a pendulum inside me. When I see God working powerfully, a voice inside me says: 'You did a great job.' Pride rises within me and all sorts of imaginings flood into my mind. Now that is Satan trying to tempt me to take the credit that belongs to God, for he knows that if I undertake my work as some ego trip its power will vanish. That is what he wants. Such thoughts need to be actively resisted in the name of Jesus.

Now this pendulum inside does not only swing one way. At other times I may have spent time praying with someone and got nowhere, and after it is all over another voice within me says: 'You're no good—if someone else had prayed with him it would have been entirely different.' A cloud of worthlessness descends and I feel I will never be able to pray with anyone again. That too is the work of Satan, who wants to crush me so that I give up stepping out in faith with God.

The prophet Isaiah says: '"I am the Lord; that is my name! I will not give my glory to another or my praise to idols"' (Is 42:8). God is jealous of his own glory and therefore will only release his power through those who are humble and will not take to themselves the praise that belongs to him.

When you recognize that we probably all live with a pendulum inside, you will be aware of the extremes and learn to take the right corrective action. I often use these words from a song of Andrae Crouch as a prayer when pride is surging within:

> Just let me live my life,
> Let it be pleasing Lord to Thee;
> And should I gain any praise
> Let it go to Calvary.
> To God be the glory
> For the things He has done.

I am thankful for feelings of worthlessness because they drive me back to God. The devil wants to destroy me with feelings of inadequacy, but God is ready to redeem every failure. Paul says of himself: 'Not that we are competent to claim anything for ourselves, but our competence comes from God' (2 Cor 3:5).

As you walk in faith and humility you will be able to keep bringing that pendulum back to the middle point of stability.

The humility of Jesus

Jesus said: 'Come to me, all you who are weary and burdened, and I will give you rest. Take my yoke upon you and learn from me, for I am gentle and humble in heart, and you will find rest for your souls' (Mt 11:28–29).

Jesus is our example of humility and it was seen in every area of his life: his life brought glory to God the Father; his teaching brought life and peace into the hearts of those who listened to him. Humility is never self-centred. It always points away from itself; Jesus's life pointed to his Father and his love reached out to others.

It says of Jesus in Philippians 2:7–8 that he made himself of no reputation, taking the very nature of a servant…he humbled himself. Do you defend your reputation? Jesus did not. A humble person is not too concerned with his reputation in the eyes of others. When Jesus was invited to eat in the house of a prominent Pharisee, he observed how the guests picked the places of honour at the table, and he considered it to be sufficiently serious to tell a parable about the importance of humility. It ends like this: 'For everyone who exalts himself will be humbled, and he who humbles himself will be exalted' (Lk 14:11).

On the night before he was crucified Jesus washed the disciples' feet in an act of deep humility. In those days, that was normally the job given to the lowest ranking servant in the whole house. Jesus deliberately chose the humblest task to show his disciples that if they were to follow in his steps they would need to be prepared to become nothing in the eyes of others (Jn 13:1–17).

A. W. Tozer writes:

> The humble man cares not at all who is greater than he, for he has long ago decided that the esteem of the world is not worth the effort. He develops toward himself a kindly sense of humour and learns to say, 'Oh, so you have been overlooked? They have placed someone else before you? They have whispered that you are pretty small stuff after all? And now you feel hurt because the world is saying about you the very things you have been saying about yourself? Only yesterday you were telling God that you were nothing, a mere worm of the dust. Where is your consistency? Come on, humble yourself, and cease to care what men think' (A. W. Tozer, *The Pursuit of God*, reissued by STL/Kingsway Publications, 1984).

Humility produces servanthood

Jesus said: 'whoever wants to become great among you must be your servant, and whoever wants to be first must be slave of all. For even the Son of Man did not come to be served, but to serve, and to give his life as a ransom for many' (Mk 10:43–45).

The incident that prompted that reply from Jesus in Mark's Gospel came as a result of James and John asking Jesus for the best seats in glory. This brought forth an indignant response from the other disciples as each one probably thought he was a more eligible candidate! The reply Jesus gave took them all by surprise.

When considering potential leadership I always look for a

person with a servant heart. It is not the glamorous roles that are the test, but the thankless menial jobs. I usually call this the 'leaf-sweeping test'. At The Hyde in autumn the quantity of leaves that fall is enormous and sometimes when I am seeking to illustrate what it means to have a servant heart, I ask: 'Would you be willing to sweep up leaves here at The Hyde as your work for God and to seek nothing greater?' It is difficult to reply with complete honesty.

A servant heart is in fact received from God by a revelation from him, as on the surface it would seem to bear no relationship to development in leadership. It is then tested in real life and if it is genuine both you and others will know that it has happened.

I found my own servant heart being tested in an unusual way. In January 1980 I travelled with Colin Urquhart to South Africa. My role was simply to pray and support; I was not involved in any teaching or preaching. What I discovered was that no one really understood why I had come. As we travelled around, Colin was the important person and at times I was almost ignored. I remember one place we visited where after two days, just as we were about to leave and were saying goodbye, our hosts had forgotten my name. Rather than glamour, here was humiliation. I went back to the Lord in prayer and was led to examine all the Scriptures that speak about being a servant; in fact, I selected a new colour and began to mark them in my Bible. That time for me was an important 'leaf-sweeping test'.

The reason for this is that in the Fall, man was infected by the Satanic aspiration to be equal with deity. This is clearly seen in unregenerate mankind which is constantly trying to elevate itself above God. It infects us all and even among Christians is expressed in the desire for advancement and recognition. Paul E. Billheimer wrote:

> This is why God uses for his greatest purposes only meek people, people that have been broken, emptied of themselves, delivered from their unholy ambition to remove God from the throne. This is why it has been said that whole, unbruised, unbroken men are of little use to God' [Miller]. Because the world worships success, sometimes the only way God can break us is by failure. This may

be a surprise to some, but God is more interested in the worker than the work (Paul E. Billheimer, *The Mystery of His Providence*, Kingsway, 1983 p.67).

Servanthood is not merely part of the promotion process, but is just as important for those who have already attained positions of responsibility and leadership. When I was in business, I made it a principle of my management that I would not ask anyone to do anything I was not prepared to do myself. That did not mean that once I had done it I was glad not to have to do it any more, but that I was ready to do it at any time. I found that this created a willing response in those who worked for me.

On the other hand, servanthood does not mean that the leader should get tangled up with tasks that others should be doing. I have seen ministers running around like errand boys with their people feeling neglected and unwanted because they were never asked to do anything.

Humility is always approachable

'People were also bringing babies to Jesus to have him touch them. When the disciples saw this, they rebuked them. But Jesus called the children to him and said, "Let the little children come to me, and do not hinder them"' (Lk 18:15–16).

The quality of approachability seen here in Jesus meant that mothers could bring their babies to him unafraid of any rebuff. The disciples were indignant, probably because they thought Jesus was far too important to be taken up with such trivial matters. The need a person is expressing to you is the most important thing in their life and needs to be treated as such. To brush them aside with a comment like: 'You don't need to worry about that' can often make the problem worse and will indicate rejection.

When Jesus was on the way to see Jairus, who had called him to heal his dying daughter, he was not so preoccupied that he overlooked the woman who reached out to touch him. Even though her healing was completed the moment she touched his cloak, Jesus stopped to turn to her with a word of faith and encouragement (Mk 5:21–43).

It is at times of pressure that approachability is tested. Do you sweep through the sea of need on your way to the next appointment? Or are you always available to answer the cry of help that comes at the most inconvenient moment?

This is where spiritual sensitivity is most important. You need to be able to hear God's priorities so that you are not so weighed down with the unimportant that you cannot respond to the unexpected, but crucial, situation.

Humility is a mark of godly wisdom

'Who is wise and understanding among you? Let him show it by his good life, by deeds done in the humility that comes from wisdom' (Jas 3:13).

James is linking together wisdom and humility as he contrasts earthly wisdom with spiritual wisdom. The former is full of selfish ambition, envy and every evil practice, because the world applauds a man who succeeds at the expense of other people. There is no such rat-race in the kingdom of God.

God's wisdom 'that comes from heaven is first of all pure; then peace-loving, considerate, submissive, full of mercy and good fruit, impartial and sincere. Peacemakers who sow in peace raise a harvest of righteousness' (Jas 3:17–18).

Two important qualities are found here. The first is an ability to listen: to be considerate, submissive, impartial and sincere indicates that all the details of the situation have been heard and responded to. The other quality is action: peace-loving, full of mercy and good fruit. Godly wisdom not only listens to the needs but takes action that solves the problems. The result is described as bringing about 'a harvest of righteousness'.

There is strength as well as sensitivity in godly wisdom.

Humility produces a caring attitude

As we proceed you will see how the various qualities we are looking at tend to interweave one with another. They are like the facets of a diamond, each adding its own quality of light.

'Do nothing out of selfish ambition or vain conceit, but in humility consider others better than yourselves' (Phil 2:3). These words are at the beginning of a section entitled 'Imitating Christ's Humility' (in the New International Version). Jesus was more concerned with meeting the needs of others than with having his own needs met.

In looking at these qualities it may be difficult to judge where we stand. We know that we ought to be acting like Christ, and we know that the needs of others ought to be a priority—but are they?

In our community lifestyle, many of our households are extended families. In my household of eleven people, there is a simple way that will demonstrate how you fare in assessing your rating in 'caring for others'. At Sunday lunch-time you observe that there is one delicious roast potato left in the bowl after everyone is served, and being a good loving person you pick up the bowl and say: 'Would anyone like the last roast potato?'

Now, the question is what are you saying inside? Are you saying: 'I would like this last potato', or are you saying, 'Would someone else like this potato?' This is quite a revealing exercise and may indicate deeper things than your own love of roast potatoes!

'Each of you should look not only to your own interests, but also to the interests of others' (Phil 2:4). Do you rejoice when others succeed? Are you happy when God uses someone else to accomplish a certain task when it might have been you? Are you able to care for others without needing human recognition?

Humility gives God all the credit

As King David was coming towards the end of his life, he looked back over all God had done and was full of praise and gratitude. 'The Lord is my rock…in whom I take refuge, my shield and the horn of my salvation' (2 Sam 22:2–3). He then goes on to elaborate the way God had demonstrated his faithfulness through the years when David was being pursued by King Saul and living the life of a fugitive.

In verse 28 he says: 'You save the humble, but your eyes are on the haughty to bring them low.' David gave all the credit to God for the blessings he had received during his life.

When God provides some money in a miraculous way, or your work for him is growing in fruitfulness, you can tell others the good news in two different ways. On the one hand, you can give all the facts and testimonies in such a way as to create the impression in your hearers: 'What a man of faith he is!' Or you can give the same information in a way that draws forth the response: 'Praise God for his power and faithfulness!' The details will not be too different, but the impression given will be very revealing.

There is a tremendous pressure on leaders to conform and to succeed. When your work is not going well there is the temptation to paint a picture that hides the reality of the situation and which shows you up in a good light. And when God blesses abundantly it is all too easy to become proud and boastful. Paul says to the Galatians: 'May I never boast except in the cross of our Lord Jesus Christ, through which the world has been crucified to me, and I to the world' (Gal 6:14).

Humility is the passport to the kingdom of heaven

Jesus had some considerable problems with his disciples, who were often arguing about their own relative greatness. '"Who is the greatest in the kingdom of heaven?"' they asked. Jesus did not answer their question immediately, but 'called a little child and had him stand among them'. 'I tell you the truth,' Jesus said, 'unless you change and become like little children, you will never enter the kingdom of heaven' (Mt 18:3).

To become like a little child is the only way into the kingdom of heaven. The gospel does not meet us in our pride and self-sufficiency—we have to come by the way of the cross to enter the kingdom. In Jesus' day it was not the religious people who accepted the word he preached, it was the poor and outcast.

The rich young man who came to Jesus to find out how to

inherit eternal life claimed to be without fault when faced with the demands of the Ten Commandments. '"Teacher," he declared, "all these I have kept since I was a boy"' (Mk 10:20). Jesus did not challenge him on the truth of his reply, but looked at him and loved him. '"One thing you lack," he said. "Go, sell everything you have and give to the poor, and you will have treasure in heaven. Then come, follow me"' (Mk 10:21). The man went away sad, because he was not prepared to become like a little child and leave his place of human security.

Jesus went on to say in Matthew 18:4: 'Therefore, whoever humbles himself like this child is the greatest in the kingdom of heaven.' All who come to faith in Christ and enter the kingdom must humble themselves before a holy God.

It is not only important that a leader has once humbled himself in this way, but that he remains in humility; otherwise, he will not be able to lead others to the foot of the cross.

People who have attained greatness in the eyes of the world often have difficulty in receiving the gospel. You may have a church full of bank managers, stockbrokers, teachers, businessmen and local government officials, but they all have to bow the knee and come into the kingdom in the same way.

In Mark 10 after the rich young man had gone sadly away, Jesus did not run after him or modify the terms of the gospel, even though he loved him. He simply said to his disciples: 'How hard it is for the rich to enter the kingdom of God!'

The Beatitudes say: 'Blessed are the poor in spirit, for theirs is the kingdom of heaven' (Mt 5:3). The New English Bible has for me the best translation of this verse: 'How blest are those who know that they are poor'.

There is only one way into the kingdom of heaven, and that way will not be found by the proud and self-sufficient. 'For the Lord takes delight in his people; he crowns the humble with salvation' (Ps 149:4).

Humility is the mark of a leader

When Paul was giving his farewell message to the Ephesian

elders in Acts 20, he very simply stated the principles by which he lived. 'You know how I lived the whole time I was with you, from the first day I came into the province of Asia. I served the Lord with great humility and with tears, although I was severely tested by the plots of the Jews' (vv.18–19).

It may seem a dangerous thing to claim to have lived in humility, but Paul went on to state many things that had characterized his ministry among the Ephesians. He had acted fearlessly and yet lovingly. The test of his statements must be the response from the Ephesians themselves: 'When he had said this, he knelt down with all of them and prayed. They all wept as they embraced him and kissed him' (vv.36–37).

Paul's Christ-like life had made a powerful impact on the Ephesians, his leadership had generated faith, his humility had created a strong bond of love.

Humility may well create reticence

When Moses was called by God to lead the Israelites out of Egypt towards Canaan, his response may have seemed somewhat surprising for an up-and-coming leader. Moses said: 'O Lord, please send someone else to do it' (Exod 4:13).

True humility does create a reticence that needs to be carefully understood. In Numbers 12:3 we read: '(Now Moses was a very humble man, more humble than anyone else on the face of the earth.)'.

This characteristic in Moses made him approachable, so much so that when his father-in-law Jethro visited him as recorded in Exodus 18, he found Moses wearing himself out in the service of the people. Jethro brought in some godly wisdom and helped Moses to choose capable men who were able to share the load. Reticence can create a reluctance to ask others to share in the work, but leaders should be looking out for people who can operate closely with them.

Reticence is a good quality in that it comes at situations from the point of human weakness and personal inadequacy, highlighting the need for God's power and wisdom.

A person who has an inflated opinion of his own capabilities is a very limited individual. He will live in a state of constant dissatisfaction, thinking that he is not being used as he ought to be. At other times he may well involve himself in situations where he is unqualified and unsuited. That kind of person will have to be held in check or he will constantly be over-stepping the mark.

On the other hand, a reticent person needs to be encouraged to be bold and helped to act decisively. Such a man will readily live in submission to others and in dependence upon God and a growth in confidence will emerge, as it did with Moses, but it will not be arrogance or self-confidence. It will be a confidence in God.

Humble yourselves therefore...

What then do you do if you find within yourself a root of pride? The Scriptures teach: '"God opposes the proud but gives grace to the humble." Humble yourselves, therefore, under God's mighty hand, that he may lift you up in due time' (1 Pet 5:5–6).

These words were addressed to the elders and young men because the tendency to pride is always a danger at any point along the Christian path. In the Bible, the only thing we are told that God actively opposes is pride. In 1 John 2:16 (AV) we read of the three ways in which the world of sin enters our lives: 'For all that is in the world, the lust of the flesh, and the lust of the eyes, and the pride of life, is not of the Father, but is of the world.'

It was the pride appealed to by the serpent in the Garden of Eden that led to the Fall. It was not only the attractiveness of the fruit (the lust of the eyes), or its potential enjoyment as food (the lust of the flesh), but the satisfaction of making an independent decision (the pride of life) that caused Eve's downfall.

How are we delivered from pride? I have heard people say of someone: 'The problem with him is that he has a spirit of pride', the inference being that if they prayed a powerful prayer over that person in the name of the Lord Jesus then he would be set free. But you cannot set anyone free from pride.

The Bible gives the only remedy: 'Humble yourselves, therefore, under God's mighty hand, that he may lift you up in due time' (1 Pet 5:6).

Nor is there any value in entering into a false humility, fondly waiting for the due time when you will be lifted up. The man of humility is more concerned with his place before God than with his standing before men. 'Therefore stand in awe of God' (Eccles 5:7).

The humble man is not a human mouse afflicted with a sense of his own inferiority. Rather he may be in his moral life as bold as a lion and as strong as Samson; but he has stopped being fooled about himself. He has accepted God's estimate of his own life. He knows he is as weak and helpless as God has declared him to be, but paradoxically, he knows at the same time that he is in the sight of God of more importance than angels. In himself, nothing; in God, everything. That is his motto. He knows well that the world will never see him as God sees him and he has stopped caring. He rests perfectly content to allow God to place His own values. He will be patient to wait for the day when everything will get its own price tag and real worth will come into its own. Then the righteous shall shine forth in the Kingdom of their Father. He is willing to wait for that day (A. W. Tozer, *The Pursuit of God*).

16

A Man of Compassion

'Sympathy is a sin!'

'That can't be true,' I replied. 'What do you mean?'

'Jesus was not sympathetic. He never sympathized with anyone.'

'That sounds even worse, please say more,' was my puzzled response.

'Jesus did not sympathize with those he met, he had compassion on them.'

'You're just playing with words,' I countered.

'No, I'm not. Sympathy comes alongside but leaves the person unchanged. Compassion not only reaches out in love to the person in need, it also meets the need and transforms the situation.'

That was the beginning of a conversation I had with Don Double many years ago which developed into a search through the Scriptures, as Don went on to explain how the quality of compassion Jesus showed brought life and power into the lives of countless numbers of people.

A man of compassion gets deeply involved with people and their predicaments, and the willingness to do this must be at the heart of leadership. In recent years many have rejoiced as more of the life and power of the Holy Spirit has come into churches and fellowships. There has been a release of praise and worship, miracles and acts of God's power have been in evidence, and this has given hope to many needy people who have been attracted to the renewed life. Some have experienced healing and freedom, but many have been disappointed at the shallowness they have found once they have dug a little deeper, and have sometimes gone away disillusioned.

The reason people have been disappointed is that there was enough of the life of Jesus to attract them initially to the body of believers, but insufficient compassion thereafter that was prepared to face the true cost of loving. As Jesus approached the time of his suffering and death, John's gospel records: 'Having loved his own who were in the world, he now showed them the full extent of his love' (Jn 13:1). That love took Jesus to the cross to pay the full price of our salvation. For those who follow in his steps, the cost of loving will not be without its demands.

Compassion is a characteristic of God

'For God so loved the world that he gave...' (Jn 3:16). God's love was demonstrated in action. He was not merely sorry for mankind, which because of sin was headed for judgement and destruction, but he acted and has consistently acted in mercy and grace since the beginning of time. 'The Lord is gracious and righteous; our God is full of compassion. The Lord protects the simple-hearted; when I was in great need, he saved me' (Ps 116:5–6). Whenever his people cried out in their need, he swiftly intervened with love and mercy.

There are times when you might be tempted to doubt the love and compassion of God. However, if you simply think of the daily blessings that are yours you will begin to grasp something of the character of your loving heavenly Father. 'Because of the Lord's great love we are not consumed, for his compassions never fail. They are new every morning; great is your faithfulness' (Lam 3:22–23).

In Psalm 77 the fear is expressed that God may not be compassionate and the cause of his people may be lost. 'Has God forgotten to be merciful? Has he in anger withheld his compassion?' (v.9.) The fact is that naturally we deserve nothing but God's judgement against sin and if God withheld his compassion we would be lost and hopeless.

King David, as Psalm 103 shows, demonstrated that God's compassion was not merely a rescue act from the wrath of a holy God, but was an abundance of rich blessings flowing from his heart:

He forgives all my sins
and heals all my diseases;
he redeems my life from the pit
and crowns me with love and compassion.
He satisfies my desires with good things,
so that my youth is renewed like the eagle's.
(Ps 103:3–5)

Compassion is a quality of the ministry of Jesus

God showed his compassion in Old Testament times in a constant response of love and mercy towards his people. He was able to act thus in the light of the eternal act of redemption that was to take place at Calvary. But it was not only necessary that Jesus should come, destined for the cross from the moment of his birth, but that he should demonstrate the compassion of his Father in a new and dynamic way. 'For the Son of Man came to seek and to save what was lost' (Lk 19:10).

The lost state of the people of his day compelled Jesus to preach the good news of the kingdom through all the towns and villages in the area, healing every disease and sickness. 'When he saw the crowds, he had compassion on them, because they were harassed and helpless, like sheep without a shepherd' (Mt 9:36).

Having taken the lead and shown by example what God required, Jesus now sent the disciples out to follow in his steps. 'He called his twelve disciples to him and gave them authority' (Mt 10:1). Jesus was so aware of the lost condition of the people that he could not remain passive about it. He longed for a response from all those to whom he preached the gospel.

He sent out the twelve with these instructions as recorded in Matthew 10:7, 'As you go, preach this message: "The kingdom of heaven is near." Heal the sick, raise the dead, cleanse those who have leprosy, drive out demons. Freely you have received, freely give.' He went on to warn them that the message would not necessarily be greeted with joy: 'I am sending you out like sheep among wolves' (Mt 10:16). The heart of the natural man is opposed to God, so the gospel will not always be welcomed.

His compassion had an infectious quality and the seventy-two disciples who were later sent out with a similar commission were soon gripped with that same sense of urgency. This was evident from their response as they returned from their mission. Luke 10:17 states: 'The seventy-two returned with joy and said, "Lord, even the demons submit to us in your name."'

Motivation for the Lord's work is not sustained by success but by his love poured out into our hearts. Jerusalem was to be the city that rejected and crucified the Messiah, and yet Jesus wept for the people: '"O Jerusalem, Jerusalem, you who kill the prophets and stone those sent to you, how often I have longed to gather your children together, as a hen gathers her chicks under her wings, but you were not willing!"' (Lk 13:34).

The compassion of Jesus led not only to an urgency in preaching the gospel but was also the underlying principle of his healing ministry. In Matthew 14:14 we read: 'When Jesus landed and saw a large crowd, he had compassion on them and healed their sick.' If healing is ministered only because it is the fashionable thing of the moment it will be largely ineffective. Healing comes from God and flowed out of the ministry of Jesus in a river of compassion and love for the people and their deep needs. I used to wonder why Jesus wept on the way to the grave of Lazarus when he probably knew that before many minutes were to pass he would be raised to life again. I now believe that his heart of love was totally identified with the grief and trauma that was being experienced by Mary and Martha (Jn 11:17–44).

Jesus's compassion was also intensely practical. When the crowd of 4,000 came to him to be taught and to receive healing, Jesus said: '"I have compassion for these people; they have already been with me three days and have nothing to eat. I do not want to send them away hungry, or they may collapse on the way"' (Mt 15:32). Jesus's love did not cease once people were healed or had come to faith, but extended to the practicalities of food and clothing. In the church today, there has been a tendency to separate and isolate the spiritual from the practical. There are those who concentrate on social justice as an expression of the gospel, while others have swung in the other direction to focus only on the need for salvation from sin. It is not either/or but both that make up the good news of the gospel.

When Jesus speaks of the day when the Son of Man will come in his glory, he says: 'For I was hungry and you gave me something to eat, I was thirsty and you gave me something to drink, I was a stranger and you invited me in, I needed clothes and you clothed me, I was sick and you looked after me, I was in prison and you came to visit me.' The righteous are puzzled by this declaration and question its accuracy. 'The King will reply, "I tell you the truth, whatever you did for one of the least of these brothers of mine, you did for me"' (Mt 25:35–40).

Compassion is a principle of the New Testament church

The only hint we receive of the kind of committed life the newly formed church was being called to live was in the new command that Jesus gave: 'A new command I give you: Love one another. As I have loved you, so you must love one another' (Jn 13:34).

The people of Israel had been used to living in a close-knit community since the earliest days of their history, and particularly so during their wanderings in the wilderness between Egypt and Canaan when they had functioned closely within their tribal identities.

Jesus is now introducing a fresh concept, the full impact of which is yet to be realized. The new basis of love and fellowship is to be only in Christ Jesus and is not according to race or background. In Acts 2:42 we read: 'They devoted themselves to...the fellowship.' The Greek word *koinonia*, here translated 'fellowship', has the meaning of 'sharing life together'. Those first 3,120 believers were starting to live the new commandment. 'Sharing life' indicated a love and commitment to one another that issued in practical action which was more than a cup of tea at the end of a church service or the name given to a group of Christians who meet once or twice a week to have services.

The Bible narrative continues: 'All the believers were together, and had everything in common' (Acts 2:44) and in Acts 4:34 we read: 'There were no needy persons among them.' But at this stage the believers were all Jews and so the further demand of love beyond racial barriers still had to be faced. However, by the time Paul wrote his letter to the Galatians the full implications of the new commandment had been felt. 'There is neither Jew nor Greek, slave nor free, male nor female, for you are all one in Christ Jesus' (Gal 3:28).

The compassion of Jesus became part of the living experience of those early apostles as they took the gospel to the then known world. They were not delivering a cold, factual statement of Christian belief, but they came in love and their message was one of love. This is clearly illustrated in Paul's letter to the Thessalonians: 'As apostles of Christ we could have been a burden to you, but we were gentle among you, like a mother caring for her little children. We loved you so much that we were delighted to share with you not only the gospel of God but our lives as well, because you had become so dear to us' (1 Thess 2:7–8). It was Len Moules who first pointed out these verses to me when he said: 'It is not enough only to preach the gospel.' This took me by surprise at the time as I then believed that to preach the gospel was the be-all and end-all of everything.

The disciples had already lived three years with Jesus and understood that the good news of the gospel was not merely a new ideology or teaching but a living faith that came to them with warmth and love. Sent out by God they continued to bring this life-changing message with all the love of Jesus which had now been poured into their hearts by the Holy Spirit.

And so the reality of a God who intervenes continued through the New Covenant people. In 2 Corinthians 1:3 we read: 'Praise be to the God and Father of our Lord Jesus Christ, the Father of compassion and the God of all comfort, who comforts us in all our troubles.' Not only is the compassion of God sufficient for salvation and physical healing, but it is also sufficient in every area of human need and suffering. The first believers knew the cost of their faith through persecution and hardship. Later in that same letter Paul wrote: 'We are hard pressed on every side, but not crushed; perplexed, but not in despair; persecuted, but not abandoned; struck down, but not destroyed. We always carry around in our body the death of Jesus, so that the life of Jesus may also be revealed in our body' (2 Cor 4:8–10).

Paul called the Philippian Christians to imitate Christ's humility, saying: 'If you have any encouragement from being united with Christ...if any tenderness and compassion, then make my joy complete by being like-minded' (Phil 2:1–2). Compassion brings about unity and like-mindedness not because we all become monochrome in our thinking, but because our love for one another releases forgiveness and understanding. I always remember my mother giving me some advice on bringing up a family: 'All parents need to be a little bit deaf and a little bit blind when raising their children.' I suppose that is what Peter was saying when he wrote: 'Above all, love each other deeply, because love covers over a multitude of sins' (1 Pet 4:8).

This is not to modify righteousness or to excuse sin, but God requires a quality of Jesus in his people that will reproduce his life in the world today. The prayer of Jesus in John 17 was for unity and love 'so that the world may believe that you have sent me' (Jn 17:21). Today's world is more aware of the divisions of the Christian church than of the compassion of Jesus within his followers. This ought not to be. Paul delivers an impassioned plea to the Colossian believers: 'Therefore, as God's chosen people, holy and dearly loved, clothe yourselves with compassion, kindness, humility, gentleness and patience. Bear with each other and forgive whatever grievances you may have against one another. Forgive as the Lord forgave you. And over all these virtues put on love, which binds them all together in perfect unity' (Col 3:12–14).

Compassion is a call to committed love

The commitment to love as demonstrated in the New Testament church is God's call to his people today. Jesus said: 'As the Father has loved me, so have I loved you. Now remain in my love' (Jn 15:9). The disciples had seen the depth of the love Jesus had for his Father and they had experienced that love themselves as they lived and worked together with him for three years. Now they were being sent out in the power of the Holy Spirit to demonstrate the life of love they had been taught.

After fifty years of Spirit-filled ministry, the apostle John wrote about love in his first letter. The question being answered was this: how can you gauge the depth of your love for God? Here is the answer: 'If anyone says, "I love God," yet hates his brother, he is a liar. For anyone who does not love his brother, whom he has seen, cannot love God, whom he has not seen. And he has given us this command: whoever loves God must also love his brother' (1 Jn 4:20–21).

This is the crunch. Your love for God is not tested by your devotion to the church, your prayer life or your knowledge of the Bible, but simply by your love for others.

The reason I live in a community is not just because I think it is a good idea. Indeed, if I could get around the Scriptures and avoid the kind of life that we are called to live I might well settle for something less demanding—I am not complaining though! When a person says to me: 'I am being called into community', all my negative reactions rise. It has to be the call of the gospel that leads to sharing of lives.

I should explain in a little more detail. During the past few years there have been many people who thought it would be a good idea to 'go into community'. It was the fashionable thing to do in many Christian circles, but sadly most such ideas have ended disastrously because the motive has been unbiblical and the method unworkable. There is little value in a group of people merely pooling resources and living together and, contrary to popular belief, they do not for the most part live either harmoniously or more economically.

Community for me begins with the call of the gospel, and

the demands of Scripture. We live a shared life because it provides a secure base for a group of people who share a common vision and have been called to work it out together.

God called me to share in the ministry of the Bethany Fellowship, and initially to be involved in travelling extensively with Colin Urquhart. Our community lifestyle provided a prayer base for the work; a proper support for our families; a simple way of life; a loving environment, and a place where we sought to live out the message we proclaimed.

As I have already said, we live in extended households that are based around a nuclear family with the addition of single people. The households are grouped into cells that meet weekly for worship, sharing and prayer, the ministry teams also meet together to pray in the context of their work and as a fellowship we worship together on Sundays and at other times during the week. We are not a church, but have been called into being by God to be a ministering community. We exist to serve the body of Christ in this nation and beyond on a non-denominational basis, and in fact God has enriched us for this work by drawing together in one Fellowship people from almost every denominational and social grouping.

The basic reason for our community lifestyle is in order to live out the command of Jesus to 'love one another'. In 1 Thessalonians 4:9 we read: 'Now about brotherly love we do not need to write to you, for you yourselves have been taught by God to love each other.' We have no right to place a limitation on the extent of our love for others, and I believe every church should be living out the New Testament principles I have outlined above. We constantly receive requests from churches asking whether we can receive certain people into our community who it is believed would benefit from our way of life. There are times when it is right for certain ones to come for a few days, but my usual answer to such a question is: 'Why are you not able to find a home for him yourselves?'

The test of the depth of your love for God and your commitment to Jesus Christ is not the way in which you perform your religious duties, but whether or not your love reaches out to the needs of your brothers and sisters.

This does not mean that every household in a church community should receive other people, but it does mean that corporately you should be able to accept the challenge with which you are faced.

In the New Testament the demands of love and compassion are stated powerfully by John and Paul and also by Peter who in his first letter says: 'Now that you have purified yourselves by obeying the truth so that you have sincere love for your brothers, love one another deeply, from the heart' (1 Pet 1:22).

Compassion encourages spiritual growth and healing

I explained in Chapter 8 how God had to deal with me to deepen my love for others, particularly those who were members of my household. That work has continued.

It was the quality of true compassion that hallmarked Jesus's ministry. He did not merely empathize with people, but reached out to his Father and met their need by his mighty power.

John's first letter spells out the imperatives of following Jesus: 'Whoever claims to live in him must walk as Jesus did' (1Jn 2:6). That is quite straightforward and rather difficult to sidestep. Later on we read: 'as he is so are we in this world' (1 Jn 4:17 RSV).

So how do we love as Jesus did? I believe that it begins with that phrase 'a place in your heart'. The people to whom you have been called have to find 'a place in your heart'. The people in the parish are not simply parishioners, the people in church are not merely members, the person who is coming to see you on Wednesday is not just 'the appointment'. They are people God has given to you to love and care for.

I can sense this kind of love when I read Philippians 1:7 and 8: 'It is right for me to feel this way about all of you, since I have you in my heart.... God can testify how I long for all of you with the affection of Christ Jesus.' In 2 Corinthians 7:3 we read: 'I have said before that you have such a place in our hearts that we would live or die with you.'

This love has set no limitations and has touched the depths

of the human heart. I do not believe effective ministry can be exercised unless this kind of love has been entered into. This is a love that will confront people in their disobedience and will bring discipline as well as the salvation, power and healing of Jesus.

It will therefore only flow out of a deep security in the love and acceptance of God. Where there is a root of insecurity or rejection in the life of a leader, true compassion will not shine through for he will have great difficulty in bringing correction on account of his own fear of being personally rejected. It seems that he is loving, but his actions are always calculated to bring about a response of acceptance from the other person. He will not confront because if he is met with a refusal to receive his rebuke, it adds to his own sense of worthlessness.

The love that confronts is clearly illustrated in the encounter Jesus had with the rich young man in Mark 10 who had come to inquire how he might inherit eternal life. The conversation developed to the point where Jesus needed to put his finger on the real blockage to faith in this man's life. In verses 21 and 22 we read: 'Jesus looked at him and loved him. "One thing you lack," he said. "Go, sell everything you have and give to the poor, and you will have treasure in heaven. Then come, follow me." At this the man's face fell. He went away sad, because he had great wealth.'

Because Jesus loved him he was prepared to confront him with the truth. The man's reaction was not very encouraging, but Jesus would not change what he had said to make it more acceptable, because of the integrity of that love.

Throughout the ministry of Jesus we find that he was rejected by countless people. He himself rejected no one. Why? Because he was totally secure in the love of his Father and knew that his nature is always giving, accepting and loving, but also embodies truth, holiness and righteousness. Jesus even knew rejection from his own Father when on the cross he cried out: '"My God, my God, why have you forsaken me?"' (Mk 15:34.) But he has triumphed over rejection and is able to heal any who will reach out to him.

Jesus's teaching was unacceptable to many because it was

too demanding and uncompromising. In John 6 we read that as a result a number of disciples no longer followed him. Jesus turned to the twelve to see how they would react, and Simon Peter became spokesman: 'Lord, to whom shall we go? You have the words of eternal life' (v.68).

As you preach the words God gives they will not always be popular, because humanity does not naturally like the spiritual message that is pronouncing death to the old way of life and presenting the demands of the life of faith. But out of love for God and for the people you must give the word that comes from his heart and will penetrate the hearts of his people. Those who do not want to respond will be angered, but those who desire to follow Jesus will be changed. A message that disturbs no one, changes no one.

The Scriptures also say: 'the Lord disciplines those he loves, and he punishes everyone he accepts as a son' (Heb 12:6). The discipline that is so necessary in bringing up our natural children is just as important in bringing up God's children, and courage and compassion are required in both cases.

I have already written of the purpose God has for his children. He does not simply want people to come to a living faith in Jesus, he wants them to become mature; to reach 'the measure of the stature of the fulness of Christ' (Eph 4:13 av). This requires discipline, correction and training in righteousness, 'so that the man of God may be thoroughly equipped for every good work' (2 Tim 3:17).

I do not wish to emphasize confrontation and discipline too strongly, because it is the compassion of Jesus in the life of a leader that will draw people to wholeness and blessing. The reason I have dealt with these two factors at some length is that often the thing that prevents real growth and fruitfulness is the shortfall in love that will not confront or discipline.

I will finish this chapter with a personal testimony. Some years ago a lady came to our Fellowship for help and encouragement—we will call her Jean. She had been very badly hurt through a life of rejection which had led to depression and fear. Joyce was asked to see her regularly for a number of weeks to bring encouragement and help through prayer and through building her up in the word. But as the weeks went by Joyce realized that in order to achieve Jean's complete healing and deliverance, she needed my help and authority.

I knew this would be a challenge to my faith and I somewhat cautiously agreed. Then Joyce came out with something that took me by surprise. 'Charles, if you are not prepared to really love Jean you will never be able to help her. She will only be able to trust you and receive from you if she knows you really love her.' I understood what was being said and went to the Lord in prayer. 'Lord, will you give me your love for Jean,' I prayed.

God answered my prayer, and as the weeks went by I knew that he had made 'a place in my heart' for Jean. There were times when she found it difficult to receive, as all the rejection of the past caused her to feel that no one would really want to love her. But the love of Jesus won through, and there was great joy in all our hearts as victory and freedom were achieved. The love for Jean has remained because God's love in our hearts is not fickle, but again through that experience God taught me how to continue to open my heart in love to others.

17

A Man of Courage

I came in quite late one evening to find that Joyce had already gone to bed. As I climbed the stairs to our bedroom, I was surprised to hear voices and the sound of music from the record player. It was obvious that some of the youth fellowship that met in our home were in the sitting-room. There were other parts of the building to which they were entitled to go quite freely, but not here.

Before taking action, I inquired from Joyce as to whether permission had been given for these young folk to invade the sitting-room and discovered that no such permission had been granted. I felt angry at the liberty they had taken.

So downstairs I went, opened the door, and announced: 'The party's over, you guys. No one gave you permission to be in here. Will you please go home so that I can go to bed.'

The record player was switched off and the half-dozen or so young lads sheepishly filed out of the room, with mumbled apologies.

That was not a great act of courage on my part, but I have told the story in order to illustrate the three principles that lie behind correct decisive action that very often does require courage.

Courageous action

The first principle is a knowledge of what is right. In the above situation, I needed to establish whether a right of access had been given or not; there needed to be a united policy coming from Joyce and myself; and I also wanted to be sure that in the context of the youth work I was acting reasonably.

The second principle is a confidence in your position of

authority. For me, this was not difficult, as I was the leader of the youth fellowship whose activities took place in my home.

The third principle is a determination to carry your action through. There was no doubt in my mind as I descended those stairs that the room was going to empty and the house be restored to peace and tranquillity within minutes. And when those young people looked at my face, they had no doubts either!

You need to grasp these principles, because they are the basis for all courageous action, and if you fail to have real assurance in any one area you will not succeed in carrying the action through. If you are acting from human pressure or from a position of doubt, and you still try to press on regardless, you will undermine your own position of authority and may well fail in your assignment.

Courage is part of God's call to leaders

If within the context of your ministry you find yourself consistently unable to carry out courageous action in the face of the circumstances confronting you, you may not in reality be a leader. You may be at peace with your position of righteousness and your status as a leader; but if you live in turmoil because of your inability to act, something needs to happen. You may be misplaced or you may need to seek God for a fresh anointing of leadership.

When Paul concludes his first letter to the Corinthians he gives these instructions: 'Be on your guard; stand firm in the faith; be men of courage; be strong. Do everything in love' (1 Cor 16:13).

We are not told that these commands are specifically addressed to leaders, but they are certainly appropriate words of wisdom for those who have that calling.

Courage is born out of the knowledge of God

In Daniel 11:32 (RSV) we read: 'but the people who know their God shall stand firm and take action'. For a Christian leader, knowledge of the right action to take will only come from your knowledge of God.

The goal of your devotional life must surely be the knowledge of God. Prayer, the word of God and worship all lead to a deeper understanding of your loving heavenly Father. You do not pray merely to receive answers to your requests but to allow that living link between God and man to be strongly forged. You do not read the Bible merely to gain knowledge and amass facts about God, but to get to know the One who has written the Book. You do not worship merely because it is your Christian duty, but because you are changed as your whole being is focused on him. 'And we, who with unveiled faces all reflect the Lord's glory, are being transformed into his likeness with ever-increasing glory, which comes from the Lord, who is the Spirit' (2 Cor 3:18).

In Leaders' Weeks at The Hyde I have often asked the question: 'Whose is the loudest voice in your life?' Is it your own voice? Is it the voice of tradition? Is it the voice of human reason? Is it the voice of denominational expectations? Is it the voice of your wife? Is it the voice of an elder, church warden or deacon? Is it the voice of the church council? Is it the voice of the people? You are the only one who can give the answer.

However, when your heart is filled with the greatness and purposes of God, other voices are silenced. I have already quoted those twin verses from Proverbs which so clearly state the two pressures that are always present in the lives of leaders. I quote them again. In Proverbs 29:25 we read: 'Fear of man will prove to be a snare' and in Proverbs 9:10: 'The fear of the Lord is the beginning of wisdom, and knowledge of the Holy One is understanding.'

Paul was conscious of his obligation to please God and not men. In Galatians 1:10 he says: 'Am I now trying to win the approval of men, or of God? Or am I trying to please men? If I were still trying to please men, I would not be a servant of Christ.' You will see how important it is to learn how to listen to God constantly (see Chapter 7).

As you get to know more of God and of his word, your life will be brought into line with his holy and righteous demands. As this affects your life it will add authority to your leadership.

That is why I wrote in Chapter 8 about the way in which God calls you to live your message. In Proverbs 28:1 it says: 'the righteous are as bold as a lion'.

Courage to expose sin

The matter of sin in the unbeliever is fairly straightforward: before a man puts his faith in Christ and responds to the gospel, the Scriptures state that he is 'without hope and without God in the world' (Eph 2:12).

Sin in a Christian takes more courage to confront. First, the person who receives a word of correction must receive it as from God and recognize his sin. If this does not happen, the one who is bringing the word can face accusations that he is standing in self-righteous judgement. That is why Jesus laid down a procedure for showing a brother his sin (Mt 18:15–17).

Secondly, the person bringing correction must be certain that the sin is real and that he has the authority to expose it. He might think: 'I cannot bring that word of correction because I too am merely a fallible human being.' That is not a justifiable excuse for a leader. The truth of God's holy standards takes into consideration the fallibility of our humanity and provides both forgiveness and victory. Age is another consideration that sometimes crops up. Paul recognized this problem when he gave encouragement to Timothy: 'Don't let anyone look down on you because you are young, but set an example for the believers in speech, in life, in love, in faith and in purity' (1 Tim 4:12).

An older couple came to see me about a marriage difficulty, and as they began to unfold their story I realized that some straight talking was required. I was faced with a dilemma, for in front of me were two people who were older than I, and in many ways more experienced Christians, and I struggled with my feelings as I contemplated the next step. I knew that the truth of God was the only way to freedom, so I took a deep breath and ploughed in. What I had to say was, to my surprise, received graciously and recognized as being appropriate.

Leadership is always by example, and it is true that if you are committing the same sin you cannot expose it in someone else. That is one of the reasons why the demands on leadership are so great.

The most outstanding biblical example of exposing sin is when Nathan confronted David with his adultery and murder as recorded in 2 Samuel 12. You will note that the three principles are followed through:

1. Nathan knew the wrongness of David's adultery with Bathsheba, and neither the social climate nor the fact that David was king altered the standards that God had set.
2. Nathan knew his position of authority in that God had sent him (v.1).
3. He carried through his unpleasant task even to the extent of bringing a severe prophetic word that outlined the things that would happen as a consequence of David's sins (vv.7–12).

David repented immediately—'I have sinned against the Lord' (v.13)—whereupon Nathan was quick to pronounce forgiveness from God. You will notice that when a word comes with the authority of God, the act of repentance will recognize that all sin is primarily against God and only secondarily against the people concerned. The result is a thorough repentance that prevents a repetition of the same sin. David's prayer of repentance is recorded in Psalm 51.

We see this same courage in the life of Jesus when he drove the money-changers from the temple and ejected those who sold doves with the words: 'Get these out of here! How dare you turn my Father's house into a market!' (Jn 2:16). There was no question of indecisiveness or failure to see the task through.

It is important in leadership to seek the courage that will act rightly even when it is unpopular, and not to take the easy way out. God is always a God of redemption and when true repentance follows the courageous exposition of sin, God in his grace will restore. That included restoring David to his position of authority and leadership: 'for with the Lord is unfailing love and with him is full redemption' (Ps 130:7).

Courage to lead your people forward

'Anything for peace and a quiet life' was at one time my motto. It was a natural emotion and not worthy of one who followed Christ. Paul expresses the goal of his life in this way: 'Not that I have already obtained all this, or have already been made perfect, but I press on to take hold of that for which Christ Jesus took hold of me' (Phil 3:12).

You need to *accept* that leadership is committed to *taking* people where naturally they would not want to go, which requires courage and determination.

Look back on your own life to times of growth in both natural and spiritual terms. When did these happen? For me, they happened most often when confronted with things I did not want to face up to. I am grateful for the courage of those who would not let me remain as I was.

To bring up children is constantly to lead them where they do not naturally want to go, whether it is teaching your five-year-old to brush her teeth or helping your teenager to establish the right standards in boy/girl relationships.

Courage is required to lead people to salvation when they might be content with their unredeemed life. There was an urgency in Peter's preaching that demanded a response: 'Salvation is found in no-one else, for there is no other name under heaven given to men by which we must be saved' (Acts 4:12).

Courage is required to lead people to live in the power of the Holy Spirit when they are quite happy living in their own strength. Jesus said: 'apart from me you can do nothing' (Jn 15:5). He also said: 'But you will receive power when the Holy Spirit comes on you' (Acts 1:8).

Courage is required to lead people into discipleship when they would rather follow their own independent way of life. Jesus said: 'If anyone would come after me, he must deny himself and take up his cross daily and follow me' (Lk 9:23).

Courage is required to lead people to live holy lives because it means you have to confront them with unholiness. In

Hebrews 12:14 we read: 'Make every effort to live in peace with all men and to be holy; without holiness no-one will see the Lord.'

Courage is required to lead people to love others when they have up to the present only loved themselves. As Peter writes: 'love one another deeply, from the heart' (1 Pet 1:22).

Courage is required to lead people to attain 'the measure of the stature of the fulness of Christ' (Eph 4:13 AV) when they would rather settle down to some comfortably nominal Christian way of life.

Jesus said: 'From the days of John the Baptist until now, the kingdom of heaven has been forcefully advancing, and forceful men lay hold of it' (Mt 11:12).

Courage that leads people forward results in spiritual growth in both the led and the leader.

Courage to press on with God

The third principle of courage is a determination to carry your actions through. There are a number of things that can happen to discourage you as you press on with the vision God has given.

Often what is most needed is a bit of honest-to-goodness grit and determination. I have heard of people who, when faced with setbacks in the work of the kingdom, will say: 'Perhaps God does not want it to happen that way.' What has really happened is that the enemy has scored a victory.

Joshua must have been a very timid and shy leader and I am sure there was a great deal of reticence in him. Why else would God need to say to him four times: 'Be strong and courageous' (Josh 1:6)?

God had given Joshua the task of leading the children of Israel over the Jordan and into the promised land and he knew it would be a very demanding operation, so he told Joshua to be strong and to have courage. As the setbacks occurred, those words must have kept ringing in Joshua's ears. The promise of God came true, for as Joshua was obedient and courageous the victories were won.

The other day a minister came to see me about the situation

in his church. Over a number of years the deacons had opposed all spiritual progress, to such an extent that Alan had felt it right to accept an invitation to another church. The result of handing in his resignation was to provoke even more obstructive behaviour from the deacons. What was he to do, as it seemed that many of the young Christians could be harmed by the conflict? I inquired as to the extent of the opposition and was told that it was church meetings and deacons' meetings that were the most difficult. Alan was able to function purposefully and fruitfully in preaching and pastoring despite being weighed down by all the conflict.

'Well,' I said, 'your responsibility is for the care of the people and their spiritual growth, and as far as I can see you are able to fulfil that quite well.'

'Yes,' Alan replied, 'but it is all the other niggles and obstructions that are getting at me.'

'Right, Alan,' I decided, 'what I am going to pray for is that God will give you a spiritual bullet-proof vest so that his work is not hindered.'

Alan left me with a renewed sense of purpose for the remaining months of his ministry in that church. It takes courage to stand firm in such a situation.

The great commission that Jesus gave to his disciples was clear and direct: 'Go into all the world and preach the good news to all creation' (Mk 16:15). Jesus also cautioned them not to embark upon this task before they had been filled with the Holy Spirit and Acts 2 tells of the dramatic and powerful way in which the fulfilment of this command began. By the time Peter's first sermon had been preached there were 3,000 new believers. The zeal for the gospel continued and the next thing that happened was the healing of the crippled beggar at the Beautiful Gate. Almost immediately Peter and John were arrested and commanded not to speak or teach at all in the name of Jesus (Acts 4:18).

However, upon their release these same disciples gathered together to pray; not for protection against persecution, but for boldness to speak the word again. They did not decide that miracles must cease because they had caused such an uproar; they prayed: 'Stretch out your hand to heal and perform miraculous signs and wonders' (Acts 4:30).

The higher principle of the call of God superseded the human law which demanded that they should stop. There may not be the same level of persecution in our land today, but who is dictating the acceptable content of your ministry?

To act with courage when the going is tough builds spiritual strength.

Courage keeps you in the place of victory

'For in Christ all the fulness of the Deity lives in bodily form, and you have been given fulness in Christ, who is the head over every power and authority' (Col 2:9–10).

You have been given a place of victory and authority because you are in Christ Jesus, but the design of the enemy is to attempt to rob you of that victory. This can occur in small ways, so that over a period of time you are worn down by the steady drip of discouragement and become weary and depressed. It requires courage to stand in the victory and not yield ground. In Galatians 5:1 we read: 'It is for freedom that Christ has set us free. Stand firm, then, and do not let yourselves be burdened again by a yoke of slavery.'

Defeat can also take place in the major conflicts you have with the enemy. There is increasing evidence of Satan's power at work in the world today, even though he has no right of victory because Jesus routed him at Calvary. He has his way because God's people fail to stand on the victory ground they have been given. Paul writes in Ephesians 6:12: 'For our struggle is not against flesh and blood, but against the rulers, against the authorities, against the powers of this dark world and against the spiritual forces of evil in the heavenly realms.' He goes on to instruct his readers to stand firm against the onslaught of the enemy and to put on the whole armour of God that will enable them to do so.

In Acts 16:16–18 there is an example of how Paul and Silas dealt with this problem at Philippi. Each day as they went to pray, a girl who had a spirit by which she predicted the future shouted after them words that were in fact true, but that they discerned came from an alien spirit. Paul endured it for many days until his patience was exhausted. He then said to the spirit: 'In the name of Jesus Christ I command you to come out of her' (v. 18). Immediately the spirit left the girl, and she was liberated from the enemy's grip.

The enemy can enter in very subtle ways. Some time ago a minister and his wife from New Zealand came to stay at The Hyde for a few days. During a communion service on the Tuesday morning we were standing in praise and worship when suddenly the minister's wife collapsed on the floor. It was obviously not something physical, but a stronghold of Satan that had been exposed by the presence of God in the worship. Authority was taken in the name of Jesus and the enemy's power was bound and later, as one of the Fellowship talked in more detail to her, it became clear that this woman's Maori background had allowed the enemy access. She was set free in Jesus's name.

The presence of the oppression and activity of the enemy in these situations is often only revealed by the holy presence of God. As God's people worship and magnify him, there will be an increasing sense of his presence and power. The psalmist says: 'Yet you are holy, enthroned on the praises of Israel' (Ps 22:3, footnote).

There is a song we use that is based on the words of that psalm:

> Jesus, we enthrone you,
> We proclaim you are King.
> Standing here in the midst of us,
> We raise you up with our praise.
> And as we worship
> Build your throne—
> Come Lord Jesus and take your place.

As this happens, the enemy will be unmasked and you will need to act courageously and decisively. When you act with courage because you will not leave the place of victory, you will see a growth in authority in your life.

Courage to have faith in the most difficult circumstances

There are two kinds of circumstances that require this quality of courage. First, there is the situation that seems completely impossible, but where you are given grace to follow the pathway God has marked out for you and come through victoriously.

Such a train of events took place when Paul was shipwrecked off Malta as recorded in Acts 27. Paul was a prisoner on board a ship, being escorted to Rome because of his judicial appeal to Caesar. He had already warned the centurion and the ship owners not to sail, but they had ignored his advice and, as predicted by Paul, they were caught in a violent storm. An angel of God appeared in the night, showing Paul how the lives of his fellow passengers could be saved, and Paul boldly spoke out the plans that had been revealed: 'But now I urge you to keep up your courage, because not one of you will be lost; only the ship will be destroyed' (v.22). The details were unfolded as the crisis continued, and as the ship's company obeyed the instructions given, God fulfilled his promise, and in verse 44 we read: 'everyone reached land in safety'.

When a crisis strikes, leadership must be especially sensitive to the voice of God, who will reveal the way through to deliverance, and the people will need courage and faith to follow their leader. It is in circumstances like these that the importance of listening first to God before listening to what men have to say is so vital. The voices of fear and panic are potentially very powerful.

I am not suggesting that you are going to find yourself in situations of physical peril, but there have been situations where a church has been spiritually shipwrecked which could have been avoided had the leadership taken time to hear God and had the people stood in courage and trust.

To have courage in the face of seemingly impossible circumstances leads to deliverance.

The second set of circumstances that requires this quality of courage is when the situation does not improve and where the suffering does not end.

Paul was facing martyrdom when he wrote: 'I eagerly expect and hope that I will in no way be ashamed, but will have sufficient courage so that now as always Christ will be exalted in my body, whether by life or by death' (Phil 1:20.) The quality here displayed has often been seen in those who have been persecuted and tortured for their faith.

A more likely event in all our lives is the sudden loss of a member of our family, which can cause such grief that a permanent scar is made and spiritual weakness is sustained. However, when you are ready to hear God's word, that in all things he is working for the good of those who love him (Rom 8:28), there is a glorious way through. It will take you to a place where you can say in the words of Joseph (slightly adapted) in Genesis 50:19: 'The enemy intended it to harm me, but God intended it for good to accomplish what is now being done, the saving of many lives.'

Many of you will have read of the tragic accident that claimed the lives of the musician Keith Green and two of his children in the summer of 1982. It was a time when he was being mightily used of God, so who would not question why such a thing should happen? However the way in which his wife Melody has come through the tragedy has been remarkable and the important result has been an increase in the effectiveness of Keith's message as his call for young people to volunteer for the mission field has resounded around the globe. His anointed music has increased dramatically in popularity and impact.

As courage is displayed in the face of such circumstances, God gives peace and increases the fruitfulness of those who trust his sovereignty.

Courage is not overbearing

Paul was sometimes accused of being bold in his letters but timid when he faced the people. In 2 Corinthians 10:1 we read: 'By the meekness and gentleness of Christ, I appeal to you—I, Paul, who am "timid" when face to face with you, but "bold" when away!'

I do not believe the accusation was valid, but that there

was a graciousness and love in all of Paul's dealings with the churches that spoke the truth in a way that people were able to receive. That is not to say there will never be any disagreements or conflicts. If a leader is living his message and has a real sense of vision and purpose from God, he will act courageously and yet creatively.

In the letter that Onesimus carried back to Philemon explaining the change that had taken place in his life, Paul says in verses 8 and 9: 'Therefore, although in Christ I could be bold and order you to do what you ought to do, yet I appeal to you on the basis of love.'

18

A Man Who Sets Others Free to Serve

I was on my way to North Wales, a 400-mile journey from Cornwall where I lived. My 1937 Riley 1½-litre Kestrel Sprite had been checked over, and I had bought a large quantity of sour plums to help keep me alert while driving.

I was to spend the next three weeks as part of the team for a Children's Beach Mission run by the Scripture Union. This was my fourth year of such activity; I had taken part in two missions in Perranporth, Cornwall, and this was now my second year at Nefyn. I had enjoyed the challenge of the work, but as I drove up the road I had no clear idea of the age group with which I should work.

Whatever age group I had been given in the past I had felt inadequate, despite the leaders having spoken encouragingly of my efforts. I now pondered the various alternatives that might be open to me. Should I continue to work with the teenagers? Or should I embark on one of the younger age groups?

By the time I arrived at Nefyn, I had reached no firm conclusion. The situation I found, however, took me completely by surprise. The people who had gathered numbered about fifteen or so, whereas in my first year at Nefyn there had been about thirty-five people and I had quite happily merged in with the Holiday Club team, the title given to the work among teenagers.

As we assembled for our first team meeting the leader, David Lewis, apologized for the diminished size of the team. He then spoke some words of faith and encouraged us to see that even though few in number we were all going to have a great mission. Dai, as he was known to us, then began to go over the various details of the teams and the responsibilities that were ahead of us.

'Now, Gillian will be responsible for the Shrimps (the 5–8s),' he spoke out nonchalantly, 'Des will be in charge of the Sprats (the 9–13s) and Charles will *lead* the Holiday Club team.'

I was stunned—this was the first I had heard of it and I had not thought of leading anything! What amazed me most was that Dai had confidence in me to do the job, and that he did not even question my willingness to take it on.

I jerked my mind back to concentrate on what was happening in the team meeting. Dai was going round the group asking the various people for their team preferences and I needed to know who was to be in my team. Half an hour later I was holding my first Holiday Club team meeting and feverishly working out how I could possibly undertake such a demanding role.

As I look back, I see this as one of the most creative things that ever happened to me with regard to my development into leadership. What Dai had done was to express a confidence and trust in me that I did not have in myself. In that act of affirmation he gave me confidence to do something of which I had not thought myself capable.

I believe his action also spoke of the quality of his own leadership, in that he was prepared to take a decision to trust someone else, with no real evidence of that person's ability to carry it through. He must have observed some potential of which I was totally unaware and his action was both liberating and deeply challenging.

The responsibility of leadership

Christian leadership exists to fulfil the purposes of God. God chooses people who are guided and empowered by the Holy Spirit and gives them various responsibilities in the body of Christ in order to carry out his plan. It is not his desire that any single individual should be attempting to fulfil every responsibility, so God-given leadership will delegate, equip and enable others to move into productive work for the Lord.

The role of the leader

In Romans 12:6 and 8 we read: 'We have different gifts, according to the grace given us...if it is leadership, let him govern diligently.' Spiritual leadership is given by the Holy Spirit, and with the privilege of the gift goes the responsibility to 'govern diligently'.

In his final instructions to Timothy, Paul said: 'And the things you have heard me say in the presence of many witnesses entrust to reliable men who will also be qualified to teach others' (2 Tim 2:2).

This verse indicates a fourfold progression:
1. 'things you have heard me say'—Paul had taught Timothy;
2. 'you have heard'—Timothy had received it;
3. 'entrust to reliable men'—Timothy was to find men of quality with leadership potential;
4. 'who will also be qualified to teach others'—Timothy was to select men with the spiritual capacity not only to receive and obey the teaching, but to pass it on to others.

The leadership principle of constantly developing others to undertake responsibility will prevent violent ups and downs in church life. Regrettably, it is a fact that few churches progress over lengthy periods of time without experiencing times of blessing interspersed with times of pain and setback. The reason usually stems from the inability of leadership to train men and women to operate effectively in ministry and second-level leadership—that is, those delegated to take on pastoral responsibility for people on behalf of the leader, such as those with pastoral and teaching gifts, which will mean that caring, counselling and teaching will stem from a broader base than one individual.

In society we have come to expect a steady increase in the quality and service offered by the shops from which we buy our goods. Your local Marks & Spencer's will have succeeded in offering you variety and service with unfailing efficiency for a great number of years, and yet the personnel will have been constantly changing. The secret lies in the ability of management to recognize potential and to provide adequate training, so that up-and-coming people have the best opportunity for development. So it should be in the body of Christ.

Corporate leadership

Improvement in leadership and ministry begins at the top and it is heartening to see the number of churches that are adopting the scriptural model of corporate leadership. Whatever the church structure in which you operate, it is essential that leadership is shared.

When Paul gave his instructions to Titus he said: 'The reason I left you in Crete was that you might straighten out what was left unfinished and appoint elders in every town, as I directed you' (Titus 1:5). Peter addressed himself in 1 Peter 5:1 to 'the elders among you', which again indicates leadership plurality in each church.

Elders in Scripture are appointed and not elected, but whatever method of appointment is used there are clear instructions in the New Testament as to the qualifications of an elder (see Chapter 8). If the eldership does not fulfil biblical standards it will not exercise godly authority.

As church members recognize the eldership, their submission to it will enhance the stature of each elder and will also increase the authority of the minister. The body of believers will know that they have a group of people who operate in mutual submission and this should eliminate isolation and independence and enable the minister to concentrate on his particular strengths as others share his responsibility for leadership.

The leader of the leaders

Even with a shared leadership, there will always be a leader of the leaders and this is taught in Scripture, if only by implication. In the early chapters of Acts this responsibility falls to Peter, for in Acts 5:29 we read: 'Peter and the other apostles replied...' When Paul felt the need to consult with another apostle he went to see Peter; in Galatians 1:18 we read: 'I went up to Jerusalem to get acquainted with Peter.'

Later on the responsibility seems to move towards James. At the Council in Jerusalem in Acts 15:13 it is recorded:

'When they finished, James spoke up…' In Acts 21:18 the visit of Paul to Jerusalem is described thus: 'The next day Paul and the rest of us went to see James and all the elders were present.'

The leader of the leaders is more than merely the spokesman; he has an anointing on his life that marks out his leadership above his fellow elders. Corporate leadership is not leadership by democracy, it is leadership by those who have been called together to hear the mind of God. God anoints men not organizations.

A broadening of leadership should cause increased fruitfulness in the church. If this does not happen, a kind of Parkinson's Law comes into operation by which tasks that were previously being accomplished by one person are now being carried out by several people but with no higher productivity.

The specific gifts of a leader

In many church situations the leader of the leaders must of necessity be the minister because of denominational structure and tradition. It is therefore unfortunate that selection of clergy is not always done on the grounds of the leadership potential displayed by the candidate. In general, our expectations of a minister are neither biblical nor practical.

In a book entitled *A Strategy for the Church's Ministry* (CIO Publishing, 1983 p.101), John Tiller quotes from a vocational leaflet entitled 'Wanted: Leaders in Tomorrow's Church':

He will be a leader of the church's worship and a man of prayer, whose oversight encourages others to discover and exercise their vocation and gifts.

He will be a planner and thinker, who communicates a vision of future goals and who seeks with others to achieve them.

He will be a pastor and spiritual director, who is skilled in understanding, counselling, supporting and reconciling both groups and individuals.

He will be a prophet, evangelist and teacher, who proclaims and witnesses to the Gospel, and who makes available today the riches of the church's tradition and experience.

He will be an administrator and co-ordinator, with responsibility for the Christian management and organization of the local church's resources.

The leaflet contains a quite excellent summary of the qualifications and personal qualities required in the church's ordained ministers. When it proceeds to describe their work, however, its effect can only be to discourage all except the foolish and the conceited.

> Since this leaflet was compiled by a group of parochial clergy, it presumably sets out what they were themselves aiming to do—and who would deny that it is what many Church members still think that their clergy should be doing?
>   There is little point in writing job descriptions of this sort (either deliberately or unconsciously) because there are few people with the necessary gifts to fill them. An important objective of a future strategy must be to end the 'general practitioner' role of the clergy which is at present normally expected in the parochial ministry (John Tiller, *A Strategy for the Church's Ministry*).

No one man is capable of achieving all those laudable goals, and even if he tried, for the most part he would do all of them inadequately, not necessarily through his own fault, but because the system is unsatisfactory.

I meet a constant stream of ministers who are faced with this seemingly insurmountable problem. They would certainly identify with the words quoted by John Tiller from the Preface to *Crockford's Clerical Directory, 1980–82* that there is 'a crisis of confidence in the hearts of many ordained ministers, who work hard but are not sure that it is work which they ought to be doing'.

I always encourage ministers to identify their own particular ministry gift and give themselves wholeheartedly to it. In the dramatic growth of the New Testament church the apostles soon realized that they could very easily be side-tracked from their particular calling to being mere respondents to need. In Acts 6:2 we read: 'So the Twelve gathered all the disciples together and said, "It would not be right for us to neglect the ministry of the word of God in order to wait on tables."'

In the general narrowed expectation of a church leadership that is centred upon one man, the characteristic of that one ministry will colour the whole work. If the leader is an evangelist, there will always be new Christians coming in, but because of a weakness in pastoring there will be a fall-off. If the leader is a pastor, all will be well cared for but very few will be added, and eventually numbers will diminish. If the leader is a teacher the people will be thoroughly grounded in the word, but there may well be a tendency towards looking inwards through a lack of outreach. The problem is a narrowness of vision and a failure to see that all the ministries mentioned in Scripture should be operating in the same congregation.

Certain ministers may well have gifts that are essential to the growth of the body of believers, but are not necessarily combined with gifts of leadership. For example, you may find someone with fine pastoral skills and a powerful counselling ministry who is not a leader. If this person by virtue of his ecclesiastical position is thrust into leadership, it will create pressure within him and will also lead to uncertainty and lack of vision in the church.

The capacity of leadership

Leaders who fail to share their responsibilities place a constriction on their own work. For example, a minister may have led a congregation of, say, eighty people for many years, and there may have been a steady stream of people becoming Christians and joining the church and yet it never seems to grow larger. Why does this happen? The simple fact is that the minister himself is the limiting factor to the growth for which he longs. He has a capacity to care for eighty people and once that number is exceeded certain people suffer neglect and leave. Of course, the number does not stay rigidly at eighty and will vary somewhat, but over an extended period of years the average membership figure will be eighty. The number could as easily be forty or four hundred.

If the minister moved to a church with a smaller congregation, it would soon grow to that number and again plateau off. If, on the other hand, he moved to a larger church, the numbers would decrease. The only remedy to this situation is the broadening of genuine pastoral care and ministry which seems a simple solution and will also enable other gifts to emerge. However, the fear factor suggests that if more people are brought into active participation the minister himself may not be needed to the same extent. This is a short-sighted attitude and one that commonly causes stagnation in the body.

Some months ago I was talking to a church elder whose minister had been complaining of overwork. The matter was brought to the leadership and after much prayer and seeking God's will one of the elders volunteered to seek early retirement so that he could join the full-time staff of the church. This was greeted with joy by all concerned, including the minister. However, once the elder finished work and presented himself for duty, it seemed that the workload had vanished and the minister's need to be needed was not going to be shared with anyone else. The elder was found some routine work, but the effectiveness of that church remained static.

Are you a limiting factor in your church?

The leader as teacher and enabler

The 2 Timothy 2:2 principle is laid down in Scripture as a way to the growth of productive ministry. Paul needed to be secure in God's purposes so that he did not have to be secretive about the things he had learnt. He had taught Timothy in the presence of many witnesses so that the principles of ministry were well known.

It is all very well having a powerful ministry, but I believe that when the principles of ministry are imparted clearly and simply then others can be set free to operate in faith as well. Jesus said: 'anyone who has faith in me will do what I have been doing' (Jn 14:12). He was committed to seeing as many people as possible exercising the same powerful ministry as he did.

In order to teach and enable, you need to understand the spiritual dynamics involved so that you are not working on a hit-and-miss basis. Having imparted the principles, they will still have to be received and acted upon in faith, for the secrets of powerful ministry are not learned by rote but are taught by faith and received by faith.

The verse in 2 Timothy states that these principles are not being conveyed to all and sundry, but only to reliable men. Every leader should be committed to enabling others to exercise effective ministry, but he needs to develop spiritual discernment as to who are the reliable men. In the story that opens this book, those in my youth fellowship who emerged into useful service for God were the ones who were reliable with the paintbrush. There were always plenty of volunteers for the glamorous tasks.

It is interesting to note in Acts 6:1–7 that the deacons who were chosen to care for the widows were to be men full of the Holy Spirit and wisdom. No work is so mundane that it can be embarked upon without the anointing of the Holy Spirit. It is small wonder that one of these men, Philip, was soon to be a powerful evangelist in Samaria with the word being confirmed by miraculous signs.

Paul says that the reliability of the men chosen must go beyond individual fruitfulness to being able to 'teach others also'. The same generosity of spirit that came from Paul was passed on down the line; narrow-mindedness and fear would stop the progression.

I was greatly impressed recently when talking with Barry Austin, who is one of the British leaders of Youth With A Mission. Barry has been responsible in recent years for the running of the Discipleship Training School at Holmsted Manor near our home in Sussex. The main vision of YWAM is to train young people in evangelism, discipleship and leadership. I was asking how various ones had become leaders.

'They have all come through the Discipleship Schools and progressed through training and encouragement,' said Barry. 'Interestingly enough, four in particular whom I trained now possess more powerful ministries than my own.' Barry went on to name them and described how God was using each of them.

A person who is ready to see others advance beyond himself in power and effectiveness has a rare quality. If more leaders were prepared to enable others to this level of fruitfulness, there would be an expansiveness in the work of God that is currently missing.

Training for leadership and ministry

Scripture teaches that God's desire is that all his people should be given the opportunity to be effective in ministry. Jesus said: 'You did not choose me, but I chose you to go and bear fruit—fruit that will last' (Jn 15:16).

Not all are called to be leaders. Leadership is a gift from God, as we have already seen in Romans 12:8, and is part of the responsibility of the elders. Leadership is normally evident in those with the five ministry gifts of apostle, prophet, evangelist, pastor and teacher (Ephesians 4).

Some years ago I remember reading in the journal of the Archbishop's Council on Evangelism an article that contrasted the method by which we select and train our ministers with the system adopted in South America. It explained how in that country they look out for those in the body who are emerging with gifts of ministry and leadership and then give them training, whereas in this country we pick people who we believe have good potential, train them, and then hope they develop into effective leaders. Our hopes are not always realized.

As all are called to ministry we need to discover the best ways of enabling each person to reach their full potential.

Life itself is the principal means of training and it is a mistake to lay too great an emphasis on any formal training that may be given. Theological training is important for certain ministries; Bible Colleges and Christian training centres will be important for others. The local church needs to follow this through so that each person is being fully and suitably prepared, the manner in which we train and provide opportunity for individual fruitfulness depending largely on our concept of the church.

The deployment of leadership and ministry

There is a sharp contrast between the Levitical priestly order of the Old Testament and the expectancy in the New Testament that all will exercise useful ministry. Under the Old Covenant we have a mental picture of the priest offering sacrifices on behalf of the people, but in the New Covenant the picture changes to a group of rough and ready fishermen preaching the gospel, healing the sick and breaking bread from house to house.

To try to re-create the Old Covenant in our priesthood today is to deny the rent veil through which we as the New Covenant people enter the holiest of all, by the blood of Jesus, and become a kingdom and priests to our God.

It is important that biblical principles are recognized in the development of church life so that its manpower is used to the full. The fact that the decrease in the full-time paid ministry has led to more lay people being released fruitfully into useful service is encouraging. John Tiller says: 'Every servant of God is called to a specialist ministry—the one which employs effectively that person's particular gifts' (John Tiller, *A Strategy for the Church's Ministry* (CIO Publishing, 1983).

So there are two things today which could happen, almost by accident, to encourage a broadening in the base of ministry—one being the decline in the number of clergy and the other being the increase in the full involvement of the body. If these developments are welcomed and not institutionalized, they could be used creatively to produce growth in the life of the church, which should in due course create the need for a larger full-time ministry team.

Women in ministry

We have been examining how God wants to see fruitfulness in every Christian. I believe that the right use of each person will produce a full-orbed and effective expression of the body of Christ in each church.

Women have a unique place in the body. They usually have a sensitivity which enables them as pastoral counsellors and they are often greatly used in the prophetic gifts of the Holy Spirit, in ministering healing and in work in most areas of the church's life.

However, in God's order, the man is called to give protection to the woman in marriage and so too I believe within the body of Christ. I therefore have difficulty in accepting a woman as a leader of leaders, or as sole leader, and yet can see her value within a leadership team.

The vexed question of the ordination of women only blurs the real issues. As Michael Harper has commented: 'To ordain women will only add to the confusion; it will simply perpetuate the caste system, only include women as well as men. We shall be no better off' (*Let My People Grow*, Hodder & Stoughton, 1977). And David Watson has added: 'In our ecclesiastical thinking, presiding at the eucharist, preaching from the pulpit, pronouncing the absolution and tying the marriage knot, have been blown up out of all biblical proportion' (*I Believe in the Church*, Hodder & Stoughton, 1978).

To say that men and women are interchangeable is to deny the uniqueness of the sexes and will cripple the real development of the ministries within the body of Christ. So will the prejudiced and narrow-minded attitudes of men, from which women have often suffered—they too need to be set free in ministry.

The creation of expanding ministry

The expansion of ministry will happen when we accept biblical principles with regard to the potential of all believers. This is stated in 1 Peter 2:5 where we read: 'you also, like living stones, are being built into a spiritual house to be a holy priesthood, offering spiritual sacrifices acceptable to God through Jesus Christ'. And again in verse 9 of the same chapter: 'But you are a chosen people, a royal priesthood, a holy nation, a people belonging to God, that you may declare the praises of him who called you out of darkness into his wonderful light.'

In 1 Corinthians 12:27, the same principle is expressed but

the imagery is different: 'Now you are the body of Christ, and each one of you is a part of it.'

The expanding team

Once it is recognized that every Christian has a part to play in the work of God, leadership needs to be sensitive to the individual development of each member. David Watson (in *I Believe in the Church*) has graphically illustrated some church structures as being like a bottle with the vicar as the cork. Just as the vicar and his church council can suppress the release of the body, conversely when the vision of expanding ministry is acknowledged then leadership has the responsibility to seek out, encourage, develop and train emerging ministry.

Insecurity in leadership will prevent this development because it fears eclipse by the new effectiveness of others. The development that is needed will not simply move the jobs around, but will create a whole new level of growth. So there is no need for fear but for a greater trust in the sovereign Lord whose plan it is.

I have read somewhere that: 'A man's ministry makes way for him.' As each individual develops under God through the encouragement of leadership there will be a distinct growth in the area in which he is operating. Those with evangelistic gifts will lead the lost to salvation; those with pastoral gifts will strengthen the growth of young Christians; those who are called to encouragement will build faith and those whose gift is giving will bless the church with their generosity. The net result will not only be more involvement for all, but will also bring growth and fruitfulness.

The stature and capacity of potential ministry and leadership

In the parable of the talents in Matthew 25:14–30 we read how the man gave out the talents, not equally, but according to individual capacity. When I talk of the development of ministry, I do not suggest that everyone has the same potential because there are many who will never become leaders, and there are others who will remain all their lives in one area of activity. God calls and appoints according to his will, not relative to some career structure where everybody is expected to pass through every department.

Look out for 10-talent people of stature and big capacity who are always needing to be challenged and stretched. Care for the 1-talent person who will not hide it in the ground but will faithfully use it for God's glory. To try to curtail the 10-talent person will be just as damaging as attempting to overstretch the 1-talent person.

The scope of ministry

Young Christians developing within the body will inevitably get involved in many different activities. I do not believe any person can really find out where their specific sphere of ministry is without 'having a go' at a number of different things. Teach your people how to seek God's anointing on the work they are doing and how to recognize the confirmation that God gives by his Spirit when the right niche has been found. Leaders need to observe this development with care and recognize the emergence of anointed ministry.

How can you tell that you are in the right job? There are many misunderstandings about this, some even feeling that God wants to give each person a most difficult and thankless task and one that they themselves do not desire. I do not believe that is God's plan.

Some months ago I was taking a church weekend in Bradford, and in the middle of a seminar on leadership I pointed to a man in the front row and asked: 'What is your ministry?'

'I don't know,' was the surprised reply.

'How long have you been a Christian?' I inquired.

'About thirteen years.'

'What are you doing at the moment in the church here?'

'Nothing, I am waiting to find out what I ought to be doing,' was the somewhat dejected answer.

'In all the years that you have been a Christian, what is the most meaningful and enjoyable thing you have done?'

He thought for a moment and then replied: 'I have felt most fulfilled when being involved with a discipleship group for new Christians.'

'That's it,' I replied, 'that is your ministry. And a tremendously worthwhile and exciting ministry it is. Go to it.'

His face was wreathed in smiles and he looked as if I had given him a fifty-pound note. I turned to the minister and said: 'There's your man for the discipleship group.'

When a person discovers their place of ministry, encourage them to stick with it until God moves them on. Effective ministry operates under anointing, not by rote! Giving everyone a turn is more likely to mask the true anointing than enable it, so when an anointed leader of praise and worship emerges among you, allow him space to grow within his sphere of service; if someone has a gift for administration, do not try to turn him into a preacher.

Limitations

The New Testament teaches that every Christian is needed if the body of Christ is to function properly. In his first letter to the Corinthians, Paul writes in 12:12: 'The body is a unit, though it is made up of many parts; and though all its parts are many, they form one body.' As the argument unfolds it is clear that each person is to have a distinct, but different, role. And from the various lists given in Romans 12, 1 Corinthians 12 and Ephesians 4, the variety indicated is broad and comprehensive. Therefore, as leadership encourages involvement within the life of a local church, it is important to allow room for the whole spectrum of gifts and ministries laid down in Scripture.

This will only happen if leadership has vision and under-standing—vision that recognizes the potential growth that takes place when each person is being used to his maximum capacity, and understanding that if there is a failure to develop ministries within the body of believers the result will be stagnation and unrest.

In our denominational church structures there are certain factors that might seem to limit the breadth of this develop-ment, the major one being the type-casting that is adopted by or imposed upon the full-time ministry. However, I have yet to come across a church where, if there was a real desire to develop the full potential of the body, it has not been possible, even taking into consideration some of the rather restrictive legal requirements of certain denominations.

Setting others free to serve God

In the pastoral letters of Paul there is a wealth of instruction to Timothy and Titus to 'make full proof of their ministries' (2 Tim 4:5 AV), and to encourage others to become mature in service too.

The 2 Timothy 2:2 principle is the basis for this chapter. There is much talk about the development of gifts and ministries, but when all is said and done, is it really happening in your own sphere? It will not come into being by accident.

Set free by affirmation

An individual cannot start in a new realm of ministry until the person who has been filling that position relinquishes it. In 1 Corinthians 16:10 we read: 'If Timothy comes, see to it that he has nothing to fear while he is with you, for he is carrying on the work of the Lord, just as I am. No-one, then, should refuse to accept him.'

I can almost hear the comments that lie behind this statement, probably a letter from Corinth saying something like this: 'We only want to receive teaching and guidance from you, Paul, please don't send us one of your bright up-and-coming new lads.' Paul is not impressed; he knows the anointing on Timothy's life and so he affirms him and sends him out with his blessing. He not only tells the Corinthians where he stands, he also affirms Timothy when he writes to him: 'Don't let anyone look down on you because you are young' (1 Tim 4:12).

The story that opens this chapter demonstrates the creative nature of affirmation in my own life and ministry and it has been very important at various stages of my development under God.

I seek to follow that same principle in relation to others. Leaders need to be able to recognize potential and launch people into new and demanding situations.

Recently I needed a new secretary, and as I sat down with Sandy to ask her to take it on I could see that she was quite apprehensive. I tried to explain what was required and finished up by saying: 'Sandy, I have full confidence that you are going to be able to do all that I need. I trust you and I am looking forward to working it out, in detail as the work proceeds.' As I finished she visibly relaxed and as the weeks have gone by, that word of affirmation has been amply vindicated.

Affirmation is not flattery, but an act of faith as a result of a deliberate decision.

Set free by encouragement

Affirmation having been given before the work has begun, encouragement is needed during and after the work has been completed. Encouragement is often sadly lacking because it is thought that we must not promote pride, and as a result many soldier on in loneliness and discouragement. This is plainly a wrong state of affairs.

Paul was open and generous in his praise to the Thessalonians when he said: 'And so you became a model to all the believers in Macedonia and Achaia' (1 Thess 1:7). If you are quick to encourage you will discover that correction is much better received and acted upon.

In Proverbs 31:31 the work of the wife of noble character is considered worthy of praise: 'Give her the reward she has earned, and let her works bring her praise at the city gate.'

Set free by being dropped in at the deep end

During my Christian life I have found that the situations that have suddenly arisen and for which I have considered myself to be inadequate, have been most creative and stimulating in my walk of faith. Some of these situations in which I have found myself have arisen more by accident than by design, and often I have been given a not-so-gentle push into the deep end. As I have reached out to God, like a drowning man clutching for a life raft, I have always found him to be utterly faithful and I know that I have matured in Christ as a result.

For those who are leaders, if you are to develop in faith and authority you will need to be able to respond readily to the unexpected. As I said in an earlier chapter, faith will only grow as it is exercised.

In setting others free to grow in faith, you need to provide situations in which they can develop. If a few people are always given the demanding situations, others will not develop faith and authority beyond their present experience.

In Acts 3 Peter and John were going to the temple merely to pray when they were confronted with the lame beggar. What should they do—throw a coin in the begging bowl, or step out in faith? They jumped in the deep end of faith, and God did a mighty miracle!

Set free by being allowed to make mistakes

When you have appointed someone to a particular responsibility and it seems to go wrong, what do you do? You stand with them to see them through.

It is helpful when a person starts on something new to allow them to do the job without any pressure of needing to succeed. I will often nominate a trial period with some regular review sessions during that time and if there is a real sense of achievement and anointing the work can continue to develop, but if the reverse is true it can cease without loss of face.

However, there are many situations where extended time needs to be given to developing experience and confidence, and during this time mistakes will inevitably occur.

Jesus was not afraid of letting his disciples fail. In Mark 9 while he was still returning from the Mount of Transfiguration, the disciples were unsuccessfully trying to deliver a young boy from the grip of an evil spirit. Jesus stepped in and put the matter right, later speaking with the disciples and instructing them that this kind of ministry would only develop as they learned more about prayer.

They were not dismissed from the job, and as we get into the events recorded in Acts we discover they had learnt from their mistakes.

If you set people free to make mistakes they will quickly respond to correction and help. 'And we know that in all things God works for the good of those who love him' (Rom 8:28).

Set free by training

As ministry emerges in the body of Christ, all will require help and encouragement from the leaders, and training can take place within the church structure for most areas of ministry. Many churches begin with Discipleship Classes and seek to develop the potential of every member, and through these it will become evident that there are some whom God is calling into ministries that require more thorough instruction. There are a number of helpful correspondence courses available these days that are well designed and skilfully produced. Ministry and leadership potential needs to emerge *first* and the training that follows can then be very productive.

Again as we look into Paul's instructions to Timothy, we find a mature attitude towards training and development. In 2 Timothy 3:16 and 17 we read: 'All Scripture is God-breathed and is useful for teaching, rebuking, correcting and training in righteousness, so that the man of God may be thoroughly equipped for every good work.'

Set free through the gifts of the Spirit in worship

In the teaching given in 1 Corinthians 12 and 14 about the gifts of the Holy Spirit, it is expected that all the members of the local body of Christ will develop in the gifts. These have been given by God for strengthening, encouragement and comfort, and if they are not allowed to function the body will suffer.

They are not meant to come only through a limited number of people, as Paul teaches in 1 Corinthians 14:26: 'When you come together, everyone has a hymn, or a word of instruction, a revelation, a tongue or an interpretation. All of these must be done for the strengthening of the church.'

So when in the worship life of your church are the people free to operate in the gifts of the Holy Spirit? It is not very helpful to hide such a time away on a Wednesday night, because only part of the body is present.

How are you going about helping everyone to prophesy, as directed by Paul? In 1 Corinthians 14:31 we read: 'For you can all prophesy in turn so that everyone may be instructed and encouraged.'

You need to provide answers to these questions if the body is to be set free to reach its full potential.

As each part does its work

In Ephesians 4:16 we read: 'From him the whole body, joined and held together by every supporting ligament, grows and builds itself up in love, as each part does its work.'

As ministry and leadership emerge it is important to allow each part to do its work. There is nothing worse than being in a situation where a leader has ostensibly released many people into various areas of responsibility but is still fussing around interfering in everyone's job. As responsibility is given, an equivalent measure of authority also needs to be granted. That does not prevent the leader exercising control and direction, but it does allow the appointed person to seek anointing and godly authority within his role and responsibility.

For example, let me share how I encourage those who lead worship. I do not choose songs for the worship time at the beginning of a meeting at which I am speaking. I expect the leader of praise and worship to have spent time seeking God and preparing himself and the worship group to lead the people into joyful praise and to prepare them to respond to the word I will bring.

The whole of that meeting is under my authority, but during the time of praise and worship I stand under their authority and anointing and trust them to lead the meeting towards its required goal. As I stand to speak, the authority passes back to me and I continue to lead the people on towards the goal I believe God is desiring.

I was tremendously impressed recently when taking a church weekend in an Anglican church on the outskirts of London. As the team arrived, we were welcomed at the vicarage and shared a meal before the first meeting. However, from that moment the vicar seemed to recede into the centre of a team of people. Throughout the weekend one person after another appeared in areas of wide-ranging responsibility. It seemed too good to be true—was this just window dressing?

The crunch came during the leadership meeting on the Saturday afternoon when I asked this question: 'What would the average church member consider to be their first line of pastoral care?' I waited expectantly for the answer. 'The house group leader would be approached first, but everyone knows that they have access to the clergy.' I was delighted that here was an example of what happens when 'each part does its work'.

God has entrusted to his people the good news of his kingdom, his rule and reign in the hearts of mankind. Leaders in his church have the responsibility:

so to live in relationship with God that they are channels for his power;

so to work by the principles of his word that the reign of God touches the lives of lost humanity;

so to liberate others that the work of God grows and multiplies.

Here is a trustworthy saying:
If we died with him,
we will also live with him;
if we endure,
we will also reign with him (2 Tim 2:11–12).

Paul the Leader

A vision for Christian leadership today

by J. Oswald Sanders

This book is concerned to show what picture the Bible gives us of the apostle Paul. It gives us a pattern for the strong, sure leadership so needed in the church today. Looking at Paul's life and writings we can discover afresh the principles of church building and leadership that inspired the early church.

Nor need we be discouraged by the thought that Paul was an 'impossible saint' who was near-infallible. Even his failures have much to teach us of the way Jesus leads his people through his appointed servants.

In Paul we find a challenging example of what one man can achieve in a single generation, if he abandons himself wholly to God.

Available from your usual
Christian book supplier, or
Mail Order enquiries to:
Charisma Christian Mail Order,
P.O. Box 77, Hailsham,
E. Sussex BN27 3EF.

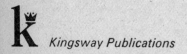

Kingsway Publications

The Furnace of Renewal
A Vision for the Church

by George Mallone

Renewal — cheap or costly?
— cosmetic or charismatic?
— passing or permanent?

Along with many others, George Mallone longs to
see renewal come to the church. But he is convinced
God is calling the church of the eighties to submit to
a baptism of the Spirit *and* of fire, so that we are
equipped and ready to play our part in God's
purposes.

*'God desires that his name be great among the nations.
To accomplish this he has chosen to refine a people to
glorify that name. His very reputation is at stake . . . It
is through the church that the wisdom of our God is
made known to principalities and powers.*

*The renewal of the church may be within reach for
those who are prepared not only to be empowered but
also refined by the Spirit.'*

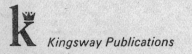

Kingsway Publications

Available from your usual
Christian book supplier, or
Mail Order enquiries to:
Charisma Christian Mail Order,
P.O. Box 77, Hailsham,
E. Sussex BN27 3EF.

Rise Up and Build

by Nick Cuthbert

How near are we to a revival in Britain today?

Can God's people move on without restoration?

What has been achieved so far by the renewal movement?

The church in Britain has entered an era that is both exciting and challenging. Christians in 'house churches' and in the traditional denominations have come into new experiences of great personal blessing.

But what are we *building?*

Nick Cuthbert brings a word of encouragement and a word of warning. He calls on churches that are weary through failure—and those trapped by yesterday's blessings—to listen to what the Spirit is saying to the churches...and then obey.

If we want the church to be an effective force in our land, let's respond to God's call today.

Nick Cuthbert is a founder of the Jesus Centre in Birmingham. He is fully engaged in an evangelistic and teaching ministry.

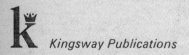

Kingsway Publications

Available from your usual Christian book supplier, or Mail Order enquiries to: Charisma Christian Mail Order, P.O. Box 77, Hailsham, E. Sussex BN27 3EF.